Where Have All Our Giants Gone?

Where Have All Our Giants Gone?

Where Have All Our Giants Gone?

STUART MILLER

TAYLOR TRADE PUBLISHING

Lanham • New York • Dallas • Boulder • Toronto • Oxford

Copyright © 2005 by Stuart Miller
First Taylor Trade Publishing edition 2005

This Taylor Trade Publishing hardback edition of *Where Have All Our Giants Gone?* is an original publication. It is published by arrangement with the author.

Published by Taylor Trade Publishing
An imprint of The Rowman & Littlefield Publishing Group, Inc.
4501 Forbes Boulevard, Suite 200, Lanham, Maryland 20706

Distributed by NATIONAL BOOK NETWORK

Library of Congress Cataloging-in-Publication Data

Miller, Stuart, 1966-
   Where have all our Giants gone? / Stuart Miller.—1st Taylor Trade Publishing ed.
      p. cm.
   ISBN 1-58979-266-1 (cloth : alk. paper)
   1. New York Giants (Football team)—Interviews. 2. Football players—United States—Interviews. I. Title.
   GV956.N368M55 2005
   796.332'64'097471—dc22

                                                        2005006289

Manufactured in the United States of America.

Contents

The Roller Coaster Era

Foreword

Dick Lynch

Looking back I can't believe how fortunate I was. Being a Giant is something you never forget. We all remember everything, starting with the pre-season workouts—in my day it was up in Vermont or Connecticut. I remember all the abuse we had to go through to get ourselves in shape; it was tough and it was brutal but it was terrific, too, because we all went through it together. That way when we went out on the football field we were out there as a unit, eleven guys together.

And that was the thing about life with the Giants, it was like being part of a family. My hat goes off to George Halas in Chicago and the Rooneys in Pittsburgh, but without a doubt the Giants are the classiest organization in the National Football League.

They were always looking for a certain type of person—not the type that was always saying "Look at me"; there'd be none of that stuff. (Even today with all the changes from the salary cap the Giants do a evaluation and they look at the man.)

The Maras were and are a pleasure to play for because they are just great people. They will always help you out any way they can and once you are a member of the Giants you are always a member of the Giants to them. That's the thing about a book like this—it tells the life story of forty different Giants covering thirty-five years, but we're all part of the same family. If we were all together each of us would look at the other and say, "Oh, he's a Giant too. I know I can count on them."

I was born in the area so my whole family was so proud to see me as a Giant, but as an announcer I saw all these players in the book who came after I retired as a player and I think that they all realized just what it meant to play for the New York Football Giants. Even when the team wasn't winning, it was different—you were not out in Kansas City or San Diego, you were here in New York and you're part of this organization. You were a Giant. It was special.

Introduction

Many New York sports fans know the basics of the Giants saga, from the Sneaker on Ice championship in 1934 to the lean years after World War II, from the championship triumph of 1956 to the heartbreaking loss in "The Greatest Game Ever Played," from the amazing run of championship-caliber teams to the aging and dismantling of that beloved roster, from "fifteen years of lousy football" to the rejuvenation that peaked with two Super Bowls in the Bill Parcells era.

Regardless of whether you grew up during the halcyon days from 1956 to 1963 or that largely dismal stretch from 1963 to 1983, every Giants fan knows the names and faces of the players they grew up rooting for—Sam Huff, Andy Robustelli, and Frank Gifford, or Baby Bulls like Tucker Frederickson and Ernie Koy, or the Crunch Bunch defense featuring Brian Kelley and Brad Van Pelt.

Yet it often seems that what we know is limited to their exploits while they were on the field wearing the uniform of Big Blue. Each player's personality is largely reflected through what they accomplished once the ball was snapped. Sure, you might have read a profile of Huff or Koy or Kelley once, years ago, but do you really know much about the childhoods that shaped them, or about their lives since their playing days ended?

I wanted this book to be different, to see these athletes as men, real people with real life stories: Buford Long segued smoothly from football to a life as a citrus farmer back home in Florida; Dick Modzelewski learned his work ethic from watching his father, who spent years toiling without complaint in underground coal mines; Ernie Koy runs a local bank just a short screen pass from where he was born; Jim Clack has survived a horrific car accident and an aggressive cancer since his playing days ended.

So how did I pick the forty players I interviewed? Readers always wonder who got chosen, who got left out, and why. To a large extent my choices were based on practical matters. The Giants organization had very little to offer in the way of contacts, but I was fortunate that some former players have kept in touch with each other. While some players told me they'd wondered whatever happened to Homer Jones, Clarence Childs knew—and gave me Homer's home phone number. No one was more helpful than Dick Lynch, who set me on my way with a dozen or so numbers, including that of his friend Tom Costello, who then provided a whole other list of names. Still, there were some players I truly wanted to interview that I simply could not find and others for whom I left numerous messages but they never called me back.

I wanted this book to be different in another way: when you look at the books—the endless parade of books—about the Giants, they invariably focus on the team from the late 1950s and early 1960s or the Super Bowl teams. It makes sense, of course, to celebrate the highlights more than the lowlights, but I think Giants fans understand and appreciate the entire history and have favorite players from each era, no matter how bad the team might have been. I grew up in the 1970s and never saw a good Giants team during my formative years but still rooted for guys like Brad Van Pelt and Brian Kelley. So I wanted to include players from each era.

I also felt it was important to include a few players who were less than household names—Tom Costello or Ken MacAfee or Bill Ellenbogen or Roy Simmons may not have had as much success on the field, but it doesn't make their lives less complete or less fascinating. I'm sure fans from those eras will remember them, and I think anyone would find their lives more than worth reading about.

So ultimately there was also a question of balance: I purposely sought out players from across the years, going back to 1947 and Gregg Browning, who might well be the oldest living Giant even though his career only lasted three games. I tracked down guys like Ben Agajanian or Bill Albright who first came to New York before the team reached its zenith. And, of course, I have plenty of players from those glorious days when the players truly were Giants—Frank Gifford, Andy Robustelli, Sam Huff, and even Roosevelt Brown, whom I interviewed just days before he died. Then there are players like Koy, Childs, and Jones from that disastrous period after Allie Sherman cleaned house in 1964, and another round of men who saw the few bright spots and the true depths of the teams in the 1970s and early 1980s, players like Ron Johnson, Dave Jennings, and Gary Shirk.

The book is set up in four sections—The Good Old Days, The Glory Years, The Downward Spiral, The Roller Coaster Era—but naturally there is overlap in each section. Ray Beck was still with the team when it won in 1956, while Roosevelt Brown arrived before then. The difference is that Brown was a building block and key player throughout the Glory Years. Allie Sherman could fit in almost anywhere—he began as a backfield coach in the Good Old Days and ran the offense and then was head coach for much of the Glory Years. But unfortunately for Sherman, he's remembered not for the great job he did for so long but for the jeers of "Goodbye, Allie" that echoed throughout Yankee Stadium after he dismantled the team in a way that led directly to the Downward Spiral.

And even within each section, you'll find there is not a pure chronological order. It's easy to begin the Roller Coaster section with Ron Johnson and Bob Tucker—they were brand-new in 1970 and key components of that season, the best year between 1963 and 1981. But beyond that it gets murky: Brian Kelley and Brad Van Pelt joined the team before Jim Clack, but they were also there after he was retired. So I've tried to create an approximate sense of chronology with an eye on flow between the chapters.

Okay, you're saying now, that all makes sense, but if I'm looking to acknowledge the lows and the highs, then what about the return to glory, the Super Bowl teams from the Parcells era? Where is Phil Simms or Lawrence Taylor or Harry Carson? Well, I left them out because I felt like this younger generation of Giants champions is still fresh in our minds and they're also still shaping their post-football lives—not that the older guys have completed their stories, but there is more of a fullness to a chapter on a sixty-something or seventy-something than a guy who is still in his early forties.

And if I get lucky, I'll get called back in a few years to do a Volume II and then it'll be time to tell their tales. . . .

The Good Old Days

G regg Browning had but the briefest of NFL careers, appearing in three games as an end for the Giants, catching just one pass before going back home to Colorado for good. But those three games took place in 1947 and now, more than half a century later, those games loom larger because Browning is one of the few men alive to have played for the Giants in the 1940s.

Still, despite his bare-bones professional career, Browning's football legacy is secure in his home state. There he coached at East Denver High School for twelve years and George Washington High School for another twelve, winning six Denver city championships at Washington, retiring with the best high school win-loss percentage in Colorado history.

"We are the only school to win a city championship the first year we opened," says Browning proudly. "I'm still very much attached to that school."

Browning grew up the son of a barber in Trinidad, Colorado, where he played football, basketball, and track in high school. He went to the University of Denver but promptly broke his hand at the start of football season and had to have the bones wired together. The school took him off the team to give him an extra year of eligibility, which worked out to his advantage in the long run, although sixty years later he still feels a slight pang of regret that he didn't get to make the team's trip to play in Hawaii in 1940. Instead, he went out for basketball and returned to football the following season.

After the 1942 season when he was named all-conference, Browning enlisted in the Navy's Air Corps. While waiting in San Diego for an assignment, he volunteered himself for the San Diego Naval Training Station. "I told the coach I could play and went out for the team on Tuesday, and I was starting that Saturday," he says. "I had such a good game that they sent me to Camp Perry in Virginia where they were gathering football players to have a good team—we played against the Washington Redskins and other service teams filled with pro players."

Browning then got his earlier wish fulfilled—in 1945, he was shipped out to Hawaii, where he was put on a Navy all-star team to play against an Army all-star team.

While he was still in the service, the Pittsburgh Steelers as well as the Cleveland Browns of the upstart All-American Football Conference drafted Browning. Browning went so far as to sign with the Browns, but after the war he decided to return to school and wanted to maintain his eligibility, so he returned the bonus to the Cleveland team.

"I had just gotten married and I wanted finish school," he says.

It was a wise move—in 1946, Browning was again all-conference and enjoyed his finest season, catching six touchdown passes. This time around, the Steelers drafted him again, but they immediately traded him to the Giants. "I thought that might happen," Browning recalls. "Mr. Mara had seen me play and said he wanted me on the team."

Browning and his wife Ruth had a great time in New York during his one season there—he still recalls the places he went with detail and relish. "We went to see plays like *Finian's Rainbow* and downtown to eat at restaurants like Luchow's, where the old-time vaudeville stars would be," he says, laughing about how the fans would loudly cheer for the "Jints." "I wouldn't have wanted to live in New York, but we really did enjoy the experience."

But one season was enough—the $6,000 gave Browning what he needed—"I just wanted to get enough money to buy a house"—and when he returned home, he got a job teaching English and coaching football at East Denver. "I loved playing and I loved athletics—if the teaching job I was hired for did not have the coaching position along with it, I would have gone back to the NFL."

Instead, Browning became a local fixture. In addition to his regular duties, at various times he pitched in coaching basketball, track, golf, tennis, swimming, and wrestling. But his heart was in teaching. "I never wanted to be in the gym. I loved the context of the whole school, of working with all the boys and the girls. These schools had high academic standards." And, of course, his heart truly belonged to football. When East Denver grew overcrowded and they moved some of the students over to the new George

Washington High, Browning became the school's first coach and brought home a title that very first year.

Along the way, Browning had offers to move up to the college level, but it never quite worked out. "The right deal never did come along," he says. There were a few tempting offers. First, he heard from the University of Colorado. He didn't want to go from being a head coach down to one of many assistants, and that assistant position paid less than his dual jobs as teacher and coach in high school. "They said I'd be traveling to do recruiting and have plenty of money in my expense account to spend, but I said that's not what I'm looking for," he says. Then the University of Denver coach Bud Blackman invited him to come along as an assistant at Dartmouth College in New Hampshire. "But I didn't want to pull up my roots."

After two dozen years of teaching and coaching in Denver, Browning thought it was "time to get my gold watch"—especially because the eldest of his three girls was about to enter high school and he thought "it would be detrimental" for the girls to be in a place where their father was so prominent. (The family soon moved to another district anyway.) So he asked to be promoted, but while he spent the next eight years as a boys' advisor in the city's junior high schools, he was always restless there. "It was a lousy job," he says bluntly.

Finally, he'd had enough, so he went to the Denver school system officials and said that he was sixty-three and was going to retire in one more year and that he "would love to coach again, someplace, anyplace." But it wasn't just anyplace—they found a spot for him as an assistant coach back at George Washington High School.

And so, it was a happy ending when Browning finally retired in 1983 . . . except . . . "I found I didn't like retirement," Browning confesses with a chuckle. So, through a friend, he reentered the athletic world through a different door, taking a job through a friend as a salesman for a chain of sporting goods stores. "But I don't like selling," he says, so he switched to working the floor in one of the stores, which was even less appealing. "That was the most boring thing I ever did, standing around waiting for someone to come in so I could show them a jock strap."

So Browning retired again, only to find that, like a heavyweight champ, "I still didn't like retirement." So he went back to his former life, reentering the school system as a substitute teacher, a job that kept him fulfilled until recently, when his wife Ruth had a reoccurrence of breast cancer. "Then I quit everything to take care of her," he says. "That was my job. I learned to cook. I learned to clean house. I didn't do anything else for a year."

It was all worth it in the end, as Ruth endured, and now, in his eighties, Browning is finally content to relax in retirement. "At my age it's nice to enjoy the memories," he says, thinking back to his college years, his brief pro stint, and particularly his time as a teacher and coach. "I enjoyed every day of it."

Ben Agajanian may be the most important kicker in NFL history that you never hear of. On the one hand, Agajanian is perfectly content with that—despite a long, storied career he seems equally proud of his accomplishments outside of football. On the other hand, Agajanian is immensely frustrated that those who should know better—the voters for the Hall of Fame in Canton, Ohio—have not recognized him.

"Bootin' Ben's" legacy does not rest on the numbers, although he nailed 273 extra points and eighty-four field goals and had seven of the eleven longest field goals that anyone had kicked to date during his career, while no other player had more than one. And he did it all back in the days, as he likes to point out, when kicks often had to be made from tough angles close to the sidelines and there was no artificial turf or domed stadiums and when the fields were often a slushy, muddy wreck by the end of the game, if not sooner.

No, the measure of fame Agajanian has earned is more historical: before him, linemen and players in other positions like Lou "The Toe" Groza were expected to perform the kicking tasks as an occasional side job to their regular football duties. Agajanian was the first pure kicker in football, the man who helped create an understanding of the importance of that role and introduce the era of specialization to a game that is now highly specialized.

Growing up, Agajanian did not have his eyes on the NFL for the simple fact that he was born in 1919, before the league itself really took shape. And, of course, back then college football relied largely on the dropkick, so there wasn't even a placekicker job to look forward to. In fact, Agajanian's well-honed kicking skills were developed not in football but first in the alleyways of Santa Ana and San Pedro, where he spent his childhood. Before he was born his father had smuggled the whole family out of Armenia, avoiding the horrible genocide going on there, and was running a refuse business and a hog-ranching business.

"The kicking all started in grammar school when I would walk to school by going down an alley and see a can and just kick it," he recalls. "I made a game of it to see if I could kick it straight down the alley. Then I would put it aside and coming home I'd go get it and kick it back down the alley. I ruined a lot of shoes that way."

With his friends Agajanian later played a made-up game called "speed ball" that involved kicking a soccer ball, and by the time he was in junior high school, the boy could send it flying for 50 yards, using the straight-on kick favored in football as opposed to the traditional soccer approach. Throughout high school Agajanian played on the tennis team but had less luck with football. In his first years in high school the football coach told Agajanian he was too light, although his junior year—when he was 5'10" but only 135 pounds—he managed to wangle a spot as a benchwarmer. His senior year he had filled out to almost six feet tall and 180 pounds, but then he found the coach was not inclined to play him anyway— "my older brother had been a wise guy and annoyed the coach, so the coach kept giving me the runaround until I said, 'The hell with it.'" (His brother, J. C. Agajanian, would go on to a life as a racing promoter, becoming "the dean" of Indianapolis racing car owners and a major figure in motorcycle racing as well.)

But while he was frustrated by his high school experience, Agajanian couldn't walk away from the game he loved. At Compton Junior College he tried out again, despite having no experience. He was woefully unprepared. "The coach asked what position I played and I had to guess, so I said tackle," he says, laughing as he remembers the skinny kid with no experience who tried to pass himself off as a tackle. "They killed me."

When the coach asked what else he could do, Agajanian was more honest and said he knew how to kick—so he was promptly sent off to practice kicking and was relegated to the sixth string, at a school with three varsity and three junior varsity squads. "There was no free substitution then, so if you kicked off you had to stay in and play," Agajanian explains of his exile. But the next year he got his chance to play for the varsity and came through, winning a big game against Pasadena in the Rose Bowl. "Pete Rozelle told me that he was in the stands that day, he was a teenager, and he became a fan of mine because I was this skinny guy who could play football," Agajanian says.

Agajanian earned himself a scholarship to the University of New Mexico, but not long after arriving he found his dreams painfully smashed. Agajanian was earning extra money in a summer job working in a Coca-Cola plant and was sitting on a barrel of syrup in a freight elevator with his foot dangling out when his foot got crushed between the elevator and a cement ledge protruding between floors. He lost four toes.

"The doctors said I would never walk again without limping and that I couldn't play football because of balance problems," Agajanian says. But while his efforts to make himself into an all-around player were clearly over, Agajanian refused to give up completely—he had the doctors even off the nubs of the amputated toes so he could kick better. Three months after his foot had healed he went out wearing three pairs of socks to fill up his shoe and started kicking. "After I kicked five or six times my foot hurt so much it got numb."

Seeing that he had no uniform in the locker room and thinking his scholarship would be revoked, Agajanian went home. But the coaches called and brought him back, saying he could just be a kicker. "I said, 'No way, it hurts too much, you'd have to get me a hard shoe.'"

The school came through for him, sending him to an old man in downtown Albuquerque who was a talented shoemaker and could create a square-fronted hard shoe. "He said, 'It's going to cost you a lot of money,'" Agajanian says. And it did: two dollars and fifty cents, which was a chunk of change during the Depression. But the school paid for it and got its money's worth, as Agajanian was soon kicking off "clear out of the end zone."

After making honorable mention all-American in his senior year, Agajanian, rated 4F for the Army because of his foot, signed with the Hollywood Bears of the Pacific Coast Pro League (PCPL) in 1942. He later enlisted anyway and was stationed in Southern California so over the next two years he could play for various PCPL teams, including the Los Angeles Bulldogs and Santa Ana Flyers. In 1945, the Philadelphia Eagles and Pittsburgh Steelers, which had merged during the war, drafted him; he eventually spent most of the season with just the reconfigured Steelers.

By this time free substitution was the rule, so he could just be a kicker, but "I was a tough little guy and I decided I still wanted to be a player," he says. And he was, making the team as a defensive end. But when he broke his arm he thought he was through. "They said, 'There's nothing wrong with your foot,' and dressed me in a uniform and sent me out." Then he kicked four field goals while his arm was in a cast and the Steelers knew they had something special. Not special enough to pay for, however—back then kickers were low, low, low on the rung, and while the Steelers wanted him back, they would only pay him $200 a game. But Agajanian had just opened his first sporting goods store in Southern California, and, considering that the Pacific Coast teams would pay him $175 per game, he walked away from the NFL.

"It was not about making history as a kicker," he says. "I thought my family and business and home were more important than kicking that damn football. I didn't realize I was doing something no one else could do."

But it was more than that. In the end, Agajanian says he is "more proud" of his business success than his life as a kicker—he eventually ended up with eight sporting goods stores, he built the Long Beach Athletic Club, and he invested and made millions in oil. "I partnered with some oil executives and bought in when oil was $2.50 a barrel and I sold out when it was up to $11.50 a barrel—I should have held on longer but I took the money and invested $500,000 of that in real estate," he says.

But while he wouldn't turn his back on his business for football, he could never leave the game entirely. The Los Angeles Rams wanted him to come kick field goals but to let Bob Waterfield handle the extra points, but Agajanian didn't like being treated as a second-rate add-on. So, he played with the Los Angeles Dons of the All-America Conference (AAC).

Settling for a field goal was, in those "man's man" days, considered to be a sign of failure by the offense and an interruption to the offense's flow, so Agajanian remained a remarkable exception. In 1947, no kicker in the AAC or NFL had more than seven field goals except for Agajanian, who had fifteen. In 1949, when the AAC folded and the Giants and Redskins both invited him back to the NFL, he went to the Giants but was frustrated by Steve Owen's lack of interest in field goals. "He didn't want a kicker. We'd be on the 30-yard line and he'd say to kick it into the corner out of bounds, so I quit."

Back in California, Agajanian oversaw his flourishing business and was perfectly content until Waterfield retired and the Rams came requesting his services. The thirty-four-year-old kicked for Los Angeles in 1953 but retired after pulling a hamstring. Then Wellington Mara stepped into the breach again, with Owen on his way out in favor of Jim Lee Howell. Mara told Agajanian he didn't have to stay with the team during the week but could fly home to check on his business between games.

After a strong year, Agajanian spent the entire next season in New York with the team, but before 1956 he decided to expand his business and retire. Mara asked him to at least come to training camp and teach Frank Gifford and Don Chandler his kicking technique. Mara even offered to pay him, which was unusual because players didn't get paid for training camp back then.

"But then Frank kicked a field goal attempt into our center's ass and afterward he goes to Wellington and says, 'I can't do everything,'" so Mara asked if he'd come back, even as a commuting kicker. And so the reluctant star returned to New York, where he had his weakest season in terms of field goals but still contributed to the championship. (He missed only one extra point in his four-year run in New York.) Now Agajanian had truly made his mark, giving birth to the kicker as specialist.

Eventually kicking went from the ninety-eight-pound weakling of pro football to the eight-hundred-pound gorilla, with the field goal becoming so prevalent and critical that those in power worried that the touchdown was becoming devalued or less desirable—that's why in 1974 they moved the goalpost back to the back of the end zone and decreed that missed field goals resulted in the ball going out to the line of scrimmage. Some have suggested calling these changes "The Agajanian Rules."

He retired after the 1957 season but returned to Los Angeles in 1960, then shuttled back and forth between two ex-Giants assistants in 1961, serving time for both the fledging AFL Dallas Texans team with Tom Landry and the Green Bay Packers with Vince Lombardi. (What happened was that Green Bay essentially borrowed him, thinking that Paul Hornung was headed to the service. When that didn't happen, neither team wanted to let him go, so he would show up in different cities in different uniforms each week, appearing in three games for each team.)

The two highlights were winning another championship ring with Green Bay and making his wife's wish come true in Dallas: she told him that for her birthday she wanted him to kick a record field goal. Now forty-two, he nailed a 51-yard field goal, setting a Cotton Bowl record. "When I made it, my wife blew me a kiss, so I blew one back to her and everybody in the stands blew one back to me," he says.

The next year Agajanian decided to help out Oakland, playing for free because they had no budget and he didn't need money. After another year away from the game he returned one more time at age forty-five in 1964—he was playing for the AFL's San Diego Chargers, but he agreed to fly out to Kansas City to help Lombardi out and coach Hornung with his kicking. When he returned to action that Sunday, the time away took its toll and Agajanian pulled his hamstring badly enough to finally end his career once and for all.

His kicking career, that is, but not his life in kicking. From 1964 until 1989, Agajanian served under former teammate Tom Landry as the kicking coach for the Dallas Cowboys. At first he was the only person with such a job, but later it became commonplace. (At first he just helped out in training camp, but his responsibilities later expanded.)

Meanwhile, he also began running the Ben Agajanian Kicking Camp, which had begun inadvertently during his career—to keep in shape during the off-season Agajanian would go to a local high school and kick, only to find himself spending just as much time giving pointers to curious youngsters there. That led to free local clinics done on a regular basis. Then, in 1974, one of his son's roommates at Thousand Oaks College said the coach had promised that Agajanian, who was nearby teaching the Cowboys, would provide instruction. Agajanian said sure, why not, and the camp was born.

Among his protégés through the years are more than forty kickers who have gone on to at least Division I football, as well as top NFL kickers like Rafael Septien, Efren Herrera, and Brad DeLouiso. (One of his four children, Larry, played football at UCLA and was drafted by Green Bay before injuring himself, but at 6'5", 265 pounds, he was better suited to the defensive and offensive lines than following his father's footsteps.) Agajanian was also an innovator: he taught centers how to better snap for the holders; he was the first to get his holders to turn the laces of the football to the front. He did it to take pressure off his toes, but it also got the ball to carry farther. He pushed for offensive linemen to use the double bump blocking to cut down on potential blocked kicks. And while the generations that followed Agajanian's retirement aroused the ire of many traditionalists with their soccer-style kicks, Agajanian welcomed them and worked on ways to improve that technique instead of converting them to straight-on kicking. When the soccer-style kickers came of age, he was the first to implement "the three back and two over," the three steps back and two over that is now a standard pre-kick ritual.

Agajanian gets riled up when discussing the Rodney Dangerfield syndrome that still afflicts kickers. "Who gives a damn about a kicker?" he complains, adding that Jan Stenerud is the only kicker in the Hall of Fame. "I don't get recognition I think I deserve."

Still, in his mid-eighties, Agajanian is not about to sit around and sulk. He's involved in his local community, sitting on local boards of businesses and banks, and he still teaches kicking. Recently, he called some kids who had not arrived for his kicking camp to remind them that there was no refund for no-shows. When he found out he had reached a Native American school in northern Arizona and that the kids had dropped out because they'd had to get summer jobs, Agajanian sprang into action. "I drove 850 miles in one day to get there, then the next day I gave the school's football coaches a clinic from eight to twelve and then in the afternoon I taught the boys. It was supposed to just be those two but the coaches brought out six kickers," Agajanian says. Knowing not to push himself too hard at this age, he stayed over in a hotel that night. But the next day he got up and drove the 850 miles back to California. Mission accomplished.

Most Giants, from just about any era, buy into the whole experience—they love being part of Big Blue, they see themselves as a member of the extended Mara family. Bill Albright never felt that way. He was born in Wisconsin and he has returned home to Wisconsin, and his link to the Giants ended in a way that foretold the modern sports era—he jumped to another team to get more money—except that in Albright's era that extra salary really was a matter of making ends meet. Although he loved his teammates, in his own straightforward and honest way Albright feels little sentimental attachment to the team.

"I really liked my teammates, but our coach, Jim Lee Howell, was a tall pain in the ass, as were the Maras," Albright has been quoted saying.

Albright was raised in Racine, playing football, basketball, and track in high school. He chose the University of Wisconsin, which offered a scholarship, so he could stay close to home. There he threw the shot put and played offensive tackle as a junior and defensive tackle as a senior, earning recognition as a *Look* magazine all-American selection that year.

The Giants drafted him, offering $4,500. When he asked for more money, Albright says he was essentially told to take it or leave it. Albright made the team as an offensive lineman in 1951, but by his third year he had switched to the defensive line full-time. After living in the Concourse Plaza Hotel his first year, he moved out to Long Beach, Long Island, where he and about ten teammates would carpool in together.

But while his salary had climbed to $5,000 in his third year and $6,500 in his fourth, Albright felt he deserved and needed more money. The Maras sent him a letter saying, Albright says, "that if I thought I could do better I should go ahead."

This time, Albright made his move, jumping to the Canadian Football League with teammate Billy Shipp when Toronto general manager Harry Sonshine began throwing money around to lure American players north. "As long as I'm getting the stuffing beaten out of me I thought I ought to get some money for it," Albright says, pointing out that his salary soared to $11,000. "The quality of play was not as good in Canada so it was nowhere near as tough. But they had the right attitude—win, lose, or draw you should enjoy yourself."

Albright played three years in Toronto and then retired, but when Montreal lost its guard to a broken leg, Albright came back for one year with the Alouettes (during which he actually hurt his own leg).

Albright had always returned home in the off-season, making it difficult to find jobs, but after his career ended he never looked back, never returned to the world of football. He found a job working for Standard Oil doing pesticide sales, but that was just a job. He discovered more inspiration up north when he and his wife Ellie (now married for more than half a century) then bought a small resort in Shell Lake, Wisconsin. "We love it here, the people are great," he says, adding that after splitting time between there, Crescent, Minnesota, and Corpus Christi, Texas, for years, he now lives there full-time.

In addition to the resort, Albright served briefly as the town's zoning administrator in the early 1970s. That role he soon tired of, leaving the part-time gig after four years because his efforts to control growth around the lake were thwarted by developers and other politicians. "There was too much pressure," he says. (His views have since been justified by flooding and sewage problems all around the lake that have led to "a really huge mess," with expensive homes under six feet of water and taxes rising to siphon out the overflow.)

But Albright found his niche in a job working for the county in social services. "I went from a killer of bugs to a social worker," he says, adding that his job was setting up supportive home care to help his elderly caseload stay out of senior housing and continue living at home. "It was quite a change but I really enjoyed it."

Now retired, Albright jokes that at seventy-five someone soon will have to help find him support services and that "I've already bought cemetery plots and the undertaker has my money." But he's far too active for that to ring true. While he doesn't fish as much as he used to, he still takes to the air with great frequency. Albright is a pilot—his two sons are pilots too—and he is also president of the Lake Point Area Club. If he isn't winging off to a "fly-in" breakfast at a small airport somewhere in the state, spending $100 for "the most expensive pancakes in the world" (the events are usually fundraisers), then you might find him mowing the lawn or shoveling the snow at the airport, helping keep his little patch of Wisconsin just right.

The saddest thing in sports is not when a player has his career cut short by injury. No, it's when that player then finds himself at a loss, unable to cope with life without the fame, fortune, and physical satisfaction brought by athletics. It's an all-too-common tragic narrative in the sports world.

Running back Buford Long suffered just such an injury—after just a little more than two seasons with the Giants, Long was permanently sidelined with a back injury that plagues him to this day. But fortunately, when it comes to Long's tale, there's a sweet ending . . . literally. This was not a guy who was lost without football. This was a guy who knew just where he was going after the cheering stopped—he was going back home, to the orange groves from where he came. And fifty years after his career ended, Long is as busy and content as ever.

Long grew up in Lake Wales, Florida, earning all-state acclaim in high school as well as a local sportswriters' award for best all-around athlete, given his play at first base and in the broad jump, high jump, and shot put. But football was his passion, and the University of Florida in Gainesville was to become his home away from home—from the moment he attended his first college game, Florida versus Georgia, he knew that's where he wanted to be. Most Saturdays in autumn that's still where you'll find him.

Long was Florida's last three-sport letterman and would have gone for four—"I played baseball and football and did track but the coach wouldn't let me play basketball"—but football was what earned him his place in the school's Sports Hall of Fame. He played three seasons, scored twenty-five touchdowns, and helped avenge the Gators against Georgia. Before 1952, Florida—which had never been to a bowl game—had won only once against the Bulldogs in their previous eleven meetings; in fact, they'd lost by 6–0 and 7–6 in Long's first two seasons. But in his senior year, the Gators broke loose with a 30–0 slaughter of Georgia, capped by Long's 77-yard touchdown run. The win propelled the Gators into their first bowl game ever, the Gator Bowl, where they beat Tulsa.

His college stardom inspired the Giants to draft him. "I was just a small-town boy and I was in awe of the big city," he recalls, adding that he lived at Concourse Plaza with Kyle Rote, Charley Conerly, Frank Gifford, and others. "It's certainly something I'll never forget."

Long plunged right into the thick of things in his rookie season of 1953—though he ran only twenty times for 58 yards, he also caught fourteen passes for 220 yards, returned seven kicks for 198 yards, and even played some defense, intercepting three passes for 59 yards. The following year, Long added punt returns and contributed 945 yards of total offense, most of it on kick returns.

But in the 1954 season, Long's career suddenly ended when he got tackled in the middle of his back. It was a legal hit, but it was in the wrong spot at the wrong time and it ruptured two discs at one time. "I could tell right away I had really hurt it," he remembers.

Long says that today doctors could fuse the discs, which would have possibly allowed his return—the doctors then told him that any more football could result in a permanently disabling injury—but would at least have reduced the risk of a life of intermittent pain. "Doctors back then didn't operate like they do today and I spent a lot of time in traction," he says, adding that while he was spending extensive periods in traction he was told that surgery as they performed it in the 1950s would cause more trouble with scar tissue than it was worth. "But I still have trouble with my back today."

But while the experience was certainly painful, it was not the end of the world for Long. He knew where home was and he knew what he wanted to do. Although his father had been in the dry cleaning business, Long says, "I grew up right in the middle of an orange grove. I knew it my whole life."

Over the past five decades, Long has had orange and grapefruit groves in and around Wauchula—as much as 1,500 acres' worth at one point, and since the early 1980s he has been the owner and operator of Buford Long Citrus. But that wasn't enough for Long—he also owned a farm equipment business for nearly thirty years, selling tractors to local farmers. "I was quite a large dealer for a while," he says. He had to fold that company after two straight bad winter freezes damaged the crops so badly "that people around here couldn't afford new tractors—I went from selling 150 in a year down to 11 and then down to 9."

Long, who has four children and four grandchildren, could have ducked some of that fiscal responsibility by simply declaring bankruptcy but says that while "that would have been the easy thing to do, I would not do it—I put mortgages on my groves and paid off all my bills."

Long's groves continue to earn their keep, although he has had to sell off and cut down to about five hundred acres after bad seasons. But Long, who also raises cattle, has always found a way to keep the business he loves and knows best going—usually in a way that will give him pleasure too. "I work because I still have to work for a living, but my wife Sammie works with me and we enjoy what we do and we enjoy life," he says.

About thirty years ago, while Long was in Las Vegas, he was approached by MGM and asked if he'd want to help organize trips and bring people from his area out to gamble. "They knew I knew a lot of people locally," he says. "Right then orange prices were pretty low so I said yes. It has been a good way to supplement our income during tough times."

Long has since shifted from MGM to the Hilton and then to Harrah's Entertainment Corporation, where he is a regional director. The work not only pays well, he says, it is fun. "I have made some lasting friends through that job." Long does seem well suited to the work, given how active he is locally—he has been on the board of the local First National Bank for thirty years and is now the chairman. And he is extraordinarily involved with his alma mater, where he is a very visible booster, with one of the original skyboxes at the stadium. "I go to all the home games and some road games too," he says.

Long has remained a Giants rooter too—the only times he found his heart torn were in the 1960s when the Giants would go head-to-head with Green Bay, led by his former offensive coach Vince Lombardi (who had filled his coaching staff with former Giants). "My teammates always teased me and said I was Lombardi's pet, but I just worked hard and did what he wanted us to do," Long says.

And when Frank Gifford organized a birthday party for Wellington Mara in 2003, while much of the attention was on the attendance of Giants stars and Hall of Famers, Long made sure to be there too. "Frank really put on a show, it was fantastic," he says. The day after the party, the players were given uniform jerseys with their names on them and introduced at the game to the crowd as Giants one more time. "That is something I'll cherish the rest of my life," Long says.

Bill Austin's voice still gets excited when he starts talking about football. The former offensive lineman played football and basketball and threw shot, discus, and javelin for the track team. (He once won the shot and placed second in the discus in state competitions.) But football was always his favorite, for a simple reason:

"You could go and hit someone hard and it was all legal," he chuckles.

Although today Austin is content living the quiet life of the retiree in Las Vegas, in the beginning he couldn't be held back; he was just bursting to get on with life. As a young child growing up in the small town of Woodburn, Oregon, Austin was always tagging along after his two older brothers, to the point where—like Mary's famous little lamb—he wanted to follow them to school. "I hollered and created such ruckus at home that my parents took me to school and told them I was six when I was only four," he recalls, adding that he was very big for his age.

Austin added muscle to his heft by working on farms every summer, pitching hay and cleaning barns. His small town had a tiny high school—only 210 kids total—so he participated in all three sports (playing both ways in football) before winning a scholarship to Oregon State University at age sixteen. (He'd graduate college by twenty.) At Oregon State the youngster was suddenly going head-to-head with much older students, full-grown men returning from World War II and going to school on the GI Bill. But Austin hails from a Navy family (his father was a chief machinist's mate for twenty-five years) so he was raised not to give up, and, of course, he had always been one to try to keep up with his brothers, so he wasn't intimidated. In fact, he was a starter on the offensive line for all four years of college, earning all-coast honors at tackle in 1948 and winning a spot in the 1949 East-West Shrine Game and in the first Hula Bowl game.

Austin wasn't thinking about a career as a player—he got a degree in human biology ("kind of like pre-med") but was contemplating the possibility of being a college coach (he'd later serve one year as an assistant at the University of Kansas at Wichita) before being drafted by the Giants.

Austin took a train by himself across the country to the training camp at Saranac Lake. He made the team in 1949 and stayed for seven years, not counting the two he missed during the Korean War. Although he was small for the offensive line, Austin was also exceptionally quick. "I wasn't that tall for a tackle but there weren't many linemen who could outrun me," he says.

Austin had a "good career" until 1954, when the Giants got a new offensive coach who would implement what is today known as "the Green Bay sweep," a running play that took advantage of Austin's quickness. That coach was Vince Lombardi.

"At camp one year everybody was wondering who the hell this little Italian guy screaming at everyone was," Austin recalls. "We soon found out."

The New York Giants of the 1950s were like a factory, producing seventeen players who would go on to life as a head or assistant coach in the NFL. One reason for that remarkable feat was that the team's two assistant coaches, Tom Landry and Vince Lombardi, understood the game and how to impart its nuances to players better than anyone. One of Lombardi's protégés was Austin, who, after that brief college coaching stint in Kansas in 1958, would ultimately follow the big man to Green Bay—he's the only living link to that coaching staff—and later to Washington, where he would even take over as head coach after Lombardi's death. Austin's coaching career would ultimately bring him back to where he first learned what he needed to be a coach, to New York, where he worked for the Giants and the Jets before retiring.

"Vince had told me he'd hire me if he ever got a job," Austin recalls, adding that when Lombardi finally got the Green Bay job and called to ask if Austin was still interested, Austin responded, "How soon do you want me there?"

As the Packers' line coach, Austin shaped Forrest Gregg, Jim Ringo, Jerry Kramer, and Fuzzy Thurston into a unit that worked together brilliantly. But while Austin got to be part of the "great story" that emerged in Green Bay, he didn't last till the Super Bowl era. Lombardi was a big believer in commitment to the team, right down to the idea that the players and coaches should live in Green

Bay. "It was a great family town," Austin recalls. But it was also freezing in winter. While Austin says he grew accustomed to shoveling his way out to go to local events, his wife Goodrun (to whom he has been married since 1956) wanted warm weather, and he decided to seek greener pastures in California. After the 1964 season, when Austin declared he was going to Los Angeles to work for the Rams, Lombardi tried to stop him, forcing Austin to go the NFL commissioner's office to be set free.

After Los Angeles, Austin was awarded the head coaching job of the Pittsburgh Steelers in 1966. It was far from a fulfilling experience. "It was very tough for me," he says. "There was not very much talent." Austin found the Rooneys constantly coming up short in financial commitment. "We didn't have too much of a chance to win."

At one point the Steelers acquired a reserve linebacker from Detroit who had been injured during the 1967 season, only to turn around and put him on waivers because, Austin was told, "we can't sign him, we're too far apart." The player was put on waivers and snapped up by Minnesota for $100. Wally Hilgenberg then went on to play for more than a decade as linebacker for the Vikings. By that time, Austin was long gone, fired after two mediocre seasons and a dreadful 2-11-1 year in 1968.

One of his most pleasurable wins along the way had come in the last week of the 1968 season when his struggling team topped the Super Bowl–bound Packers. "I think they were overlooking us," he says, adding that Lombardi was so furious, he didn't even come into his dressing room after the game to visit. "One player told me he kept them in there for an hour and a half afterwards and the next week was the hardest week they ever had."

Lombardi was obviously impressed with what Austin was doing with what little he had, and when he went on to coach the Washington Redskins he hired Austin to help run the offense. Soon after, however, the legendary coach died and, still pulling the strings from the hospital before he went, appointed Austin as his successor. (Former Giants teammate and Rams head coach Harland Svare was on hand to help run the defense.) "It was a big surprise but it was what he wanted," Austin says.

But it wasn't easy. The team was shocked by Lombardi's death and stumbled in 1970, finishing at 6-8, and Austin was gone. Still, he worked after that as an offensive assistant with a good, no-nonsense reputation for another decade and a half, including five years under Ray Perkins with the Giants, a couple of years with the United States Football League's New Jersey Generals, and a brief stint with the Jets—as their third offensive line coach in four years—hired by another former Lombardi assistant, Joe Walton. After losing that job when the quarterbacks were sacked a league-record sixty-two times in his one season—part of the blame certainly belonged to Ken O'Brien, who held the ball far longer than most passers—Austin retired. "I was a little tired of coaching by then," he says, "and I was getting a player's and a coach's pension till the end of my life."

Austin moved back to California, where he briefly owned the Sixth Avenue Mail Station in downtown San Diego, where he oversaw a business that featured mailboxes, made keys, rented videos, and sold novelty items. Then he retired to Las Vegas, where one of his three daughters was going to school and "needed some parental guidance."

Today, she works in the Las Vegas hotel business, another daughter is a schoolteacher in Alaska, and a third lives in Arkansas. His son, who is now an emergency medic, grew to be 6'3" and 215 pounds, but Austin didn't really want him playing football and getting banged up like the old man. Since retiring, much of Austin's time has been eaten up by recuperation—nine months to recover from getting a new knee, another nine months to bounce back after hip replacement surgery, more time gone to getting a pacemaker put in. Now, Austin says he needs another new knee but the doctors don't think his heart is strong enough to handle the surgery.

Still, Austin gets around fine. He does a bit of traveling—he even thinks he'll get around to going up to "the boonies" one of these days to visit his daughter in Alaska—and when he's home, he still goes to the gym to work out regularly. Despite the pain and injuries, in fact, Austin is in good shape. "I still weigh 215 pounds, what I weighed when I was playing," he says.

Ray Beck didn't grow up dreaming of playing in the National Football League the way kids do today—back then the league wasn't much to aspire to. Still, Beck played football constantly on the sandlot throughout his childhood, relishing the game's physical contact.

Small-town Georgia, like small-town Texas, had pretty much only one sport on its mind. "Growing up in Cedartown all we had was football," Beck recalls. That's not to say he didn't have other options tugging at him. Beck played the trumpet, and freshman year when he was getting set to go out for the team, the band director pulled him aside and urged him to think about his choice, trying to lure him back with the promise that "you could be first trumpet next year."

But the scrawny, 128-pound Beck was determined, and he made the team, growing to 150 pounds by sophomore year, then to 185 as a junior and 205 in his senior year. But his team went only 3-3-3 that year and, as Beck points out, "colleges didn't recruit that much in small towns, especially with losing teams."

So Beck had to go on "a tryout tour," which took him to the University of Chattanooga, which offered him a half scholarship, and to Georgia Tech, which was on its way to the Orange Bowl, coached by Bobby Dodd. "They put me on defense for practice that day and afterwards offered me a scholarship. I took it right away."

Beck, who would ultimately be inducted into the College Football Hall of Fame in 1996, earned letters for three years and started for two. He played on both the offensive and defensive lines, but he always preferred defense. The reasons were simple. "On offense you couldn't extend your arms, but on defense you could do anything," he recalls. "You could whomp them any way you wanted."

As a senior, it all came together for the 6'2", 215-pound Beck and for his team. The Yellow Jackets went 11-0-1, capturing the Southeastern Conference (SEC) championship and defeating Baylor in the Orange Bowl, while Beck was named the conference's most outstanding lineman and first-team all-American. "It was a lot of fun," he says, adding that all along he hadn't particularly thought about pro football, which was still far behind baseball and boxing in the hearts and minds of sports fans. "It wasn't televised much back then and was lucky to get two paragraphs on the back page of the sports section," he says.

Even after the Giants made him a second-round draft pick in 1952, offering him $5,000, Beck says, "I wasn't sure if I wanted to play." His uncertainty was compounded when the Montreal Alouettes of the Canadian Football League offered him $6,000. Soon he heard from the Giants, asking why he hadn't returned the contract. When Beck told them about the Canadian competition, the Maras matched the money.

Still, it was clear right away that this was far from a glamorous life, Beck says. "In your contract it said you had to bring two pairs of football shoes and one pair of tennis shoes on your own," he says, adding that when he and Frank Gifford went from the College All-Star Game in Chicago to Milwaukee to meet up with the Giants, they got thrown right into an exhibition—without any money. The first paycheck didn't arrive until the middle of September, well after the six exhibition games and the $10 a week for laundry had come and gone.

After one year with the Giants, Beck, who had been in ROTC at Georgia Tech, went off into the service during the Korean War. He played football for various Army teams, even getting transferred from one fort to another by greedy officers who wanted him for their team.

Then he went to Korea for eighteen months just as the war was ending. Although he had to carry sidearms, he never saw any action, adding, "but it was just tough to be away for so long."

By the time Beck returned, the pieces were starting to fall into place for the Giants. Beck inadvertently helped another one along when he was injured in a game against the Chicago Cardinals and missed some action, allowing a young rookie linebacker by the name of Sam Huff to show his stuff.

Winning the championship in 1956 was obviously the highlight of Beck's career, but he says he had a grand old time all along. "Being from a small town in Georgia, I was treated pretty good up in New York, going to Toots Shor's to eat on Sunday night," he says, adding that these days, with the salary cap forcing teams to get rid of top talent so quickly, a defensive (or offensive) unit never has the chance to gel together the way the Giants of the 1950s did on and off the field.

Beck almost didn't come back after '56. His father died and his mother needed help at home with the family trucking business. Then Wellington Mara called. "He asked, 'What would you play for?'" Beck recalls, still a bit shocked by the generosity all these years later. "I had never heard that before." Knowing that the top linemen in the league earned $12,000 to $13,000, Beck, who had pulled in $9,500 during that championship season, blurted out $12,500. "And Mara said yes."

Still, despite the extra money and his desire to keep playing, Beck called it quits after 1957, returning home to the family business, which he ran for thirty-four years until selling it in 1991. The business initially served only north Georgia but eventually grew to serve most of the southeast. Beck kept it based in Cedartown, although he had a big terminal in Atlanta and an agency in Macon and traveled quite a bit. "I did my own sales for a while," he says. "I liked the sales better than operations. It was tough and it was long hours."

Finally, when deregulation came, Beck saw that "you had to get bigger or get out, but as you get bigger you get more and bigger headaches, so when an offer came to buy the company, I took it." By the end, he says, "I was tired of it."

These days Beck cuts the grass and watches sports and plays golf, but he also keeps active on numerous boards, including the Georgia Sports Hall of Fame and the statewide Olympics. He was chairman of the First National Bank of Polk City until he turned seventy, when he became chairman emeritus. "I really enjoyed my ten years as director of the Atlanta chapter of the NFL Alumni association," he says, adding that in the group's charity golf tournaments he got to become friends with a lot of players from other teams he had never really known.

As for his former mates on the Giants, Beck doesn't see them much, tucked away in his hometown of Cedartown. "We all live in different places now," he says. "But we still enjoy each other when we do get together."

The Glory Years

Roosevelt Brown was the ultimate company man. The Hall of Fame offensive lineman was a member of the Giants family for more than fifty years and was the second most visible link to the team's past, behind owner Wellington Mara. And Brown was quick to tell anyone who will listen that he couldn't have found a better home.

"I was truly fortunate to come to the Giants," he said in one of his final interviews before dying at the age of seventy-one in the spring of 2004.

Born in 1932, Brown grew up in Charlottesville, Virginia, where he played trombone in his high school band until one day the school's football coach decided that any thirteen-year-old who weighed 180 pounds could find a place on the line in football. Brown's play at offensive and defensive tackle earned him a scholarship to all-black Morgan State College in Baltimore, where he played football and was a two-time wrestling captain. Brown was surprised to be drafted by the Giants in the twenty-seventh round (out of thirty) in 1953 after someone on the team noticed a listing for a 6'3", 225-pound left tackle who had just been named to the Black All-America team. It proved the wisest choice they made that year—only three of the twenty-six players chosen ahead of Brown made the team, and none ever started.

Still, Brown didn't know what to expect—he had never seen a professional game before and, in fact, had never even seen white colleges play, nor played with or against whites. "The University of Virginia wouldn't let us into the stadium," he recalled.

But the Giants, from the Mara family down to good ol' Southern boys like quarterback Charley Conerly, welcomed him and helped him adapt to New York and to the pro game. "We were all one big family. Today there would be a lot of teams I couldn't play for—coaches in the pros don't want to coach anymore. The Giants taught me how to play football," Brown said, adding that he didn't even know the proper offensive lineman's three-point stance when he arrived. He didn't even know at first that being signed didn't mean he couldn't be cut.

Not that life in the NFL was ever easy. Brown and fellow black Em Tunnell often couldn't stay with their teammates on the road, so Wellington Mara would find black families for them to stay with. Brown also used to tell a story about head coach Steve Owen getting riled up because Brown couldn't stop Len Ford of the Cleveland Browns. According to the story, Owen said if Brown couldn't block Ford, Owen would cut him, so on the next two plays Brown tackled Ford. When Ford threatened, "If you do that again I'm going to kill you," Brown responded, "If I don't stop you I'm going to get cut, so what's the difference if you kill me?"

Brown didn't get cut, of course. And in fact, there were very few guys he couldn't stop. Gifford has said that he owes his Hall of Fame success to Brown's blocking on the pitchout and the sweep; Brown's speed and ability to move downfield made him one of the few tackles ever to pull like that. Even legendary teammate Sam Huff has said he was intimidated the first time he saw the impressive Brown physique—at 245 pounds he was the third-largest Giant, but he had only a 29-inch waist. Conerly once said that Brown was probably the greatest of all the Giants greats. Coach Allie Sherman says that Brown "was one of the two greatest linemen ever to play the game," and *Sports Illustrated* said he may have been the best ever.

Brown earned invitations to ten Pro Bowls as the Giants made it to the NFL title game six times between 1956, the one time they won, and 1963. The 1956 championship game when the Giants toppled the Chicago Bears 47–7 was a highlight. "We beat the heck out of them," said the man voted Lineman of the Game. (But don't get him started on "The Greatest Game Ever Played" that the Giants lost to the Baltimore Colts in sudden death overtime in the 1958 championship. "We were cheated," he recalled, referring to the infamous play near the game's end when the refs, after an injury, placed the ball short of a first down for the Giants after Frank Gifford supposedly gained the necessary yardage. "The referees definitely made a mistake.")

By 1965, knee injuries had caused phlebitis, an inflammation of the veins that led to blood clots. In the Pro Bowl game he got hit hard, but the coaches just "wrapped me tight and like a fool I went back in. That was my last game."

That's when he really appreciated how special the Giants organization truly was. The doctor said Brown could conceivably continue playing despite the phlebitis flare-ups and subsequent suffering. But Wellington Mara said that he'd pay Brown the same amount to become a coach as he would to play. Brown, who had worked as a schoolteacher and other jobs during off-seasons, knew he wanted to stay in football, so he jumped at the chance. "Being black, I would have been out on the streets with most other teams," he said.

Brown became an assistant offensive line coach. He loved teaching, but he was turned off by the attitudes of younger players as the money began to get better. "One player told me, 'Mr. Brown, I don't give a damn about football, I just want to be able to go to the bank Monday,'" he said. By 1971, the resistance to learning combined with the pressure of his job "depending on how well someone else played" led Brown to a new role. "Wellington Mara asked if I'd stay on and become a scout." So Brown stayed. And stayed. And stayed. Until his death he was still scouting for the Giants.

Brown's job changed dramatically throughout the years. For starters, white schools wouldn't allow him in, so his first "territory" as a scout was the black schools. "It didn't change until the late 1970s," Brown said. Secondly, there was no "combine" in the spring back then to bring all the top talent together, so scouts would have to hit the road in the spring, going from school to school, and then go back in the fall during the season to reassess. And, of course, the game itself changed. "So many people today just look for size in offensive linemen," he complained. "It's ridiculous. A guy who is huge but not an athlete is going to be beaten from the get-go. I look for athletic ability and the sort of person whom I would want to coach."

In his last years Brown was semi-retired but still scouted within the region, driving to towns like Pittsburgh or Syracuse with his wife, Linda, and spending three or four days visiting a city. That's because his physical ailments made flying difficult—"I have a pacemaker and an artificial knee, so going through airports is pretty damn tough," he said.

The knee problems began after his playing days when Brown took up skiing and, one day in the Poconos in Pennsylvania, stumbled doing a jump turn coming off the lift. "I couldn't walk down, so I had to ski down on my injured knee," he said. Then the doctors botched the surgery, again and again. All told, he has had eight surgeries and he still can't bend his leg properly.

Brown also had a slight stroke in 1990, harming the left side of his body, which prompted him to muse that he might retire. Mara said he'd lose his health insurance and should instead stay on and just scout as little or as much as he wanted. Brown, who had lived and scouted in California during the 1980s, lived his final years with Linda on two and a half acres in Columbus, New Jersey, way down south in Burlington County. "I love the outdoors," he said, explaining that his strength as a player came from all the outdoor work he did as a boy in Virginia.

In fact, at one point Brown bought ten acres in Virginia where he could "garden and plant things and cut trees—I heated my house just with a fireplace and a wood-burning stove." Unfortunately, he found that Virginia had not changed much from his childhood "as far as blacks and whites go," so he moved to New Jersey, where he could work outside and grow his own vegetables. In fact, Brown was in his beloved garden when he collapsed and died.

But until the end, he also continued driving up the turnpike to Giants Stadium, where he tried imparting his knowledge of the game to each generation of Giants. Not surprisingly, he didn't just talk strategy and tactics; he also preached the virtues of Big Blue.

"I tell young players the Giants are a great organization," Brown said, looking back across his life. "Play hard and they'll do right by you. I'm a perfect example—since I left school I have never had another job away from the New York Giants."

t seems like forever, as if Frank Gifford had been in the spot-
light his entire life, and in a way it's true—all-American at
USC, the ultimate golden boy of the greatest Giants teams,
Monday Night Football, the marriage to Kathie Lee.

Yet these days the Giants legend who single-handedly inspired
the literary genius of Frederick Exley in *A Fan's Notes* has little
interest in being center stage. He's got a new role, one he's perfectly content with.

"I love being Mr. Mom," he says, explaining that he takes his
children Cody and Cassidy to school, picks them up afterward,
and attends all their events as well. "I was away long enough with
my first family—I hardly knew my kids when they were little."

In a way, it's surprising that Gifford didn't give up life on the
road earlier, after a *Grapes of Wrath* type of childhood spent bouncing around during the Depression, living in forty-seven different
towns as his father moved from one short-lived oil field job to another. As a result, Gifford tended to count his older brother Waine
as his best friend, and he also always struggled in school—in high
school in Bakersfield, living with relatives while his parents were
off in Alaskan oilfields, he even flunked wood shop.

In his sophomore year, Gifford was stuck as a third-string end
on the Sand Dabs, the school's junior varsity team, leaving him
completely miserable. He was also cutting class, scamming the attendance records to avoid trouble. In his junior year the attendance
officer, Homer Beatty, who also happened to be the football coach,
caught him. Beatty threatened to throw him out of school but instead tried to reform him; when the varsity team, the Drillers, had
their quarterback killed in a car accident, Jones made Gifford his
quarterback. It turned Gifford's life around, thrusting him into the
limelight and sending him on the path to college. Under Beatty's
guidance, the young star became a tailback, running, passing,
punting, returning kicks, doing everything and doing it well. His
senior year Gifford made all-conference and led the Drillers to the
San Joaquin Valley championship. But he also became ambitious in

his schoolwork, eventually earning the grades to match his skills on the gridiron—after a year at Bakersfield Junior College to make up for lost time, Gifford was off to the promised land at the University of Southern California (USC).

Gifford struggled at USC for a while, stuck on defense for most of his junior year, although he led one stirring comeback at quarterback. But in the season's second-to-last game he was called on in front of eighty thousand screaming fans to punt—the first time he'd ever punted in a game—from near the Trojans' goal line in a desperate effort to cling to a 9–7 lead over mighty Notre Dame. Gifford kicked the ball 75 yards, sealing the win. The following season, with a new coach, Gifford finally became the focal point of the offense (while continuing to play defensive back), and again he came through, leading the team to seven straight victories—he rushed for nearly 900 yards, caught eleven passes, completed thirty-two, intercepted three more, and kicked twenty-six extra points and two field goals. Gifford could do it all.

This was the beginning of Gifford's decades-long role as a star. (He had already been earning some extra money along the way as an extra and stunt double in Hollywood movies, kicking footballs in Jerry Lewis's stead in *That's My Boy*.) He was named Collier's all-American running back and then became a media darling, getting interviewed constantly. In the middle of that run, the Trojans had come to Yankee Stadium to play the Army team. It was a wet, sloppy game, yet Gifford rushed for more than 150 yards that day, catching the eye of a guy in the stands by the name of Wellington Mara.

But the Giants had Kyle Rote at halfback and were eyeing Gifford for defense, so although he was their top pick, they offered him only $7,500 to sign. "I had a little baby on the way and my brother-in-law wanted me to go into the building business with him," Gifford recalls. "Then I was contacted by the Canadian Football League and they offered more money."

But the $12,000 for the CFL wasn't enough to dispel the lure of the NFL, and when the Giants gave him $8,250, Gifford's future was set. (Although he was already a pro, Gifford continued commuting from Bakersfield to USC in the off-season to get the final credits needed to become a college graduate, which he did in 1956, a season of accomplishment for all the Giants.)

But when he arrived in camp in 1952, Gifford found that "no one knew quite what to do with me"—he did not have a clearly defined role, and legendary coach Steve Owen as well as many of the veterans dismissed him as a California pretty boy deserving of extra physical punishment in practice. (In his memoir *The Whole Ten Yards*, Gifford describes Owen as "a fat snarly Oklahoman who dipped snuff . . . and stuck rigidly to his old ways of doing things.") When the season began, Rote was the starter and Gifford was stuck playing cornerback and returning kickoffs. Gifford still found stardom, however, going to the Pro Bowl for his defense. "Tom Landry was the safety then and he was a big help to me," Gifford recalls.

In 1953, Gifford got his break when Rote went down with an injury, but the opportunity was a mixed blessing—the Giants were an awful team, and for the last seven games, "I played both ways and never came out," Gifford recalls, his body taking a brutal beating. "I almost didn't come back after that year, saying to myself, 'Who needs this?' But I really liked Wellington Mara and he personally asked me to return."

And 1954 would be the start of something new, with a new coaching staff on hand. Gifford still gets excited today when recounting his first conversation with the new offensive coach. "He said, 'I'm Vince Lombardi and you're my halfback,'" he recalls. The season was filled with promise as Gifford led the conference with a 5.6-yard-per-carry average, and the Giants were in first place until both Gifford and Rote got injured on the same play in week nine. For Gifford it was a knee injury that would never fully heal. (That season also witnessed Gifford branching out more into television commercials like the one for Rapid Shave.)

Although the Giants started slowly in 1955, they finished strong, including a rout of the feared Detroit Lions in the season finale. "That's when I knew we were pretty good," Gifford says. "And Vince said to me afterward, 'I got a feeling about this team.'"

The feeling was right on target. The year 1956 began with the team moving from the Polo Grounds to Yankee Stadium, where Gifford was assigned the locker of none other than Mickey Mantle. The team was dominant, ultimately routing the Chicago Bears 47–7 in the championship, and Gifford emerged as a superstar, winning the league's MVP award. It would change his life—he was suddenly earning $25,000 a year from the Giants and was also the mystery guest on *What's My Line* and modeling bathing suits in ads, among a myriad of other print, radio, and television endorsements. Two years later he was given a seven-year deal by Warner Bros., although that never led to anything more than bit parts. Reaching this elite level also propelled Gifford forward into his next career. Although he had been doing local television at home in Bakersfield in the off-season, being "The Man" in New York led to local news and even pregame network television work, all of which helped set up his gig at ABC doing *Monday Night Football*. "At the time I knew I was very fortunate," Gifford says.

The glory days nearly came to a sickening conclusion with one play in a game against Philadelphia on November 20, 1960. After Gifford caught a pass over the middle, linebacker Chuck Bednarik nailed him and nailed him hard. Gifford went down like he'd been shot, and, when the Eagles recovered his fumble, Bednarik pumped his fist in celebration. When Gifford didn't get up—he had a deep brain concussion—Bednarik looked like a villain, a role Gifford says he has milked unreasonably considering it was a perfectly legal hit. "I was off balance and my leg just snapped back but Chuck made a second career out of talking about it," he says, complaining that "the play has defined my career. It's ridiculous." (Bednarik did send him a telegram, a get-well card, flowers, and a basket of fruit in the hospital.)

The next year Gifford announced his retirement, prompted not just by the hit but by a long-term radio contract offer from CBS. Gifford stayed in touch with football by working as an advance scout for the Giants; although the press didn't know it, he even worked out with the Giants during the week. "I really missed playing," Gifford says he finally realized. The next season he returned, as a flanker, and adjusted brilliantly, becoming the first person named to the Pro Bowl at three positions and earning the Comeback Player of the Year award.

In 1964, after twelve seasons, Gifford really was done, ready to move on to a full-time job as a sports reporter for CBS. But after a few years at CBS, Gifford began aching for more responsibility—to move from sports to news, for instance, an opportunity that was not there. He didn't get to do the news, but something better did come along: Roone Arledge. Arledge offered *Monday Night Football*, along with the chance to do *Wide World of Sports*, the Olympics, and more. The producing wizard tried hiring Gifford for the first football season, but he was still under contract to CBS, but in year two he slid into the booth alongside Don Meredith and Howard Cosell, forging a persona that is perhaps even better known than the one from his football days.

"I was doing a job in the maelstrom," he says. "You'd have to swallow your ego to do play-by-play with those two—sometimes I'd have to say, 'It's third-and-three, do you guys mind?'"

(On Cosell, Gifford says, "He was self-promoting, selfish, and unusual, but interesting. He said some horrible things about me but less than he did about most people.")

Along the way, Gifford's stardom and his relentless work ethic (and need for financial security, driven by his childhood) broke up his first and second marriages. But then in 1982, while subbing on *Good Morning America*, he met Kathie Lee Johnson. For four years they were just friends, with Gifford even fixing her up on dates, but eventually, as has been well documented in the media, they fell in love and got married, weathering some notoriously public rough spots and producing two children.

Gifford left *Monday Night Football* in 1998 and now dabbles in real estate and investment deals, travels from his home in Connecticut to one of his others in Nantucket and Key Largo, and helps out Kathie Lee with her career. She often travels to California for her work, but Gifford has no desire to move back west, having long ago fallen in love with the New York area . . . and with his new, stay-at-home, out-of-the-limelight lifestyle. "Everything I do, I can do on my own time," he says.

laying for the New York Giants was a powerful, life-transforming experience, in ways you might never imagine—playing on the team in the 1950s brought fame, glory, and professional satisfaction, especially in that 1956 championship season, but for tight end Ken MacAfee, being a Giant had impact in another area, one smaller, yet more shocking. It transformed a born-and-bred Boston Red Sox fan into a lifelong New York Yankees fan, someone who sits in Quincy, Massachusetts, each October rooting for a team that can only be described as the enemy.

MacAfee came of age in Brockton, Massachusetts, during the DiMaggio-Williams era, going with his mother—a huge sports fan—to Ladies' Day and Sunday doubleheaders at Fenway Park while his father and three sisters stayed home. "I don't think my father ever took me to a game, I always went with my mother," he recalls.

Back then baseball was his passion. "Football was kind of my second love at the time," he says. "I would rather have been a baseball player."

In high school in nearby Easton he played both baseball and football, along with basketball and even track—he was the only four-letter athlete ever at the school. "I set a couple of state records in the 100-yard dash and the 220," he says. "I could always move my body."

After high school, MacAfee spent one year at Boston University before transferring to the University of Alabama. It was a move he had planned for years. As a teenager he was listening to an Alabama–Boston College game on the radio one day when he suddenly reached a decision. "My mother was ironing clothes and listening with me and I announced 'I'm going to go to Alabama,'" he says. "And I did."

At Alabama MacAfee played one year of baseball before injuring his back and focusing entirely on football, which was rapidly becoming his focal point. "They used to play exhibition games down there and I went to a Detroit Lions–Washington Redskins game in

Birmingham and I got the bug right then," MacAfee recalls. "I told this kid I was with, 'I'm going to play pro football someday.' He looked at me like I was crazy."

MacAfee's entry into the NFL was delayed by the draft—during the Korean War he spent two years in the Marine Corps, but life on Parris Island and then in Quantico, Virginia, still revolved around football. "It was a very good experience," he says. "The duty wasn't too hard. We played a lot of football. We had a great team at Parris Island—I even played with Bob Schnelker there—then I was transferred to Quantico because a three-star general who had a lousy team grabbed everybody he could. I even got to play some basketball there."

While MacAfee was in the Marines, he signed with the Giants, although he wasn't sure at first what to expect. "I was very excited, but I didn't know much about the Giants," he says. "Then when I got to camp there were seventeen ends there and I said, 'What am I doing here?'"

But MacAfee, along with Schnelker, outlasted them all. "I wasn't the greatest player in the world, but I could always block," he says. He could catch, too: he enjoyed a stellar rookie season in 1954, catching twenty-four passes for 438 yards, an average of 18.3 yards per catch, and tying with Schnelker for the team lead with eight touchdowns—only three players in the whole league had more. The sophomore slump bit MacAfee in the form of an injury, but he bounced back in that golden year of 1956 with what would be the second-best year of his career, scoring four touchdowns. "Vince Lombardi was the offensive coordinator and he came to training camp that year and said he was starting a new offense," MacAfee recalls. "I asked him, 'Do I have to wear number 70 or can I keep my number 80?' meaning, would I be just blocking or getting to catch the ball? He said not to worry, he wanted to pass. That was really the start of the tight end position as we know it today."

As the team was learning its new moves and coming together they lost virtually all their exhibition games, but when the season opened it was a different story. MacAfee's two personal highlights were catching a long touchdown pass from Frank Gifford (who had gotten the ball on a pitchout) against Washington in the season's closing weeks to help avenge one of the Giants' only defeats that year, and scoring both touchdowns for the Giants in the College All-Star Game after winning the NFL championship. "The guys gave me the ball after that game," he says. "That was really nice."

That was also the year that the Giants moved from the Polo Grounds to Yankee Stadium—the team would have to work out at Fordham University early in the season and play a slew of road games because the Yankees were always in the World Series, but it also gave MacAfee a chance to see the perennial powerhouse up close. He would watch the Yankees and the Yankees would watch the Giants. "After their season would end, Yogi Berra would have nowhere to go, so he'd come back to the stadium and watch us practice," MacAfee recalls. Something rubbed off and MacAfee's allegiance soon switched from "Red Sox Nation" to the Bronx.

His loyalty to New York would remain strong even after the 1958 season, when he was traded to the Philadelphia Eagles, one of the Giants' main rivals. "It was tough to leave the Giants," he says. "I almost cried like a baby."

Even though the Eagles literally "ripped up my contract right in front of me and gave me more money," MacAfee had a tough time getting motivated in his new environment. "I wasn't excited about going there," he says, which was compounded by what he calls "the worst training camp I ever saw. They did nothing. Everybody gained weight in that training camp."

After four games the Eagles let him go, but the Washington Redskins immediately picked him up. Still, at the end of the season MacAfee knew his time in the NFL was up. "It was time to leave," he says. "My kids were starting school and I had a good job waiting."

MacAfee spent the next few years working for Wilson Sporting Goods. First he was a collegiate sales rep, calling on colleges in the Boston area. Then he moved to Allentown, Pennsylvania, to handle the mid-Atlantic and some southern states, selling an upscale line called King O'Shea. He managed to move back home, though, taking a job with Massachusetts-based F.C. Phillips selling athletic spikes to shoe manufacturers, a job he held for twenty-nine years. Then he put in a few years handling money for a friend who owned a dog-racing track until "the day I turned sixty-five, when I said, 'Bye-bye.'"

These days, MacAfee plays in charity golf tournaments and travels with his wife, Diane. They also drive down to Florida each winter, where he plays in more golf tournaments. While there and along the way up and back, he visits with former teammates like Alex Webster, Frank Gifford, and Ray Beck. "It's a nice brotherhood," he says.

Anyone who knew Andy Robustelli back in his football days or who knows him now in semi-retirement might think it odd that a large chunk of his post-football career revolved around a travel company—after all, Robustelli was, and is, a man who likes to be close to home. His desire to be near his family is what brought him to the Giants, and these days in semi-retirement he prefers relaxing near his home and office in Connecticut to traveling. However, anyone who has ever known Andy Robustelli also knows that with intelligence and a dogged work ethic he would make a success out of just about anything he tried to do.

Born in 1925, Robustelli grew up in Stamford, Connecticut, the son of a barber and a seamstress, both of whom instilled in the aspiring football star the importance of family and hard work. He played football constantly with his friends and for his high school team as well before going into the Navy, where he served out in the Pacific Ocean for more than two years during World War II as a water tender below deck firing the boilers.

Afterward, he came home and became a two-way football star and baseball standout at tiny (and now defunct) Arnold College in Milford, Connecticut. Although the competition was relatively weak, his exploits still attracted the attention of the New York Giants baseball team and the Los Angeles Rams, who drafted him in the nineteenth round because of his punt-blocking ability, thinking he might help out on extra teams.

Baseball was his preferred sport, but signing with the Giants wouldn't mean being in New York—they wanted to ship him out to Knoxville, Tennessee, at the low Class B level of the minor leagues for additional seasoning. Already twenty-five, Robustelli was impatient to get on with his life, either in the NFL or as a teacher—he had some high school teaching offers too. So he went to LA, even though his chances of establishing himself as an offensive end on a team packed with stars like Tom Fears and Elroy "Crazylegs" Hirsch seemed daunting. Instead, he made the team as a starter on defense and immediately helped the Rams win the 1951 championship.

Robustelli would go on to become one of the game's greatest pass rushers and a leader as well—he would play on teams with winning records in every season but one. He led by example, with his impressive work ethic—he did miss one game that rookie season, but that was something that would never again happen to the iron man in fourteen NFL seasons. Jim Brown once called Robustelli and Gino Marchetti the two "toughest" guys in the league.

Robustelli eventually grew tired of having his family on one coast and his job on the other. Before the 1956 season he asked the Rams if he could report to camp late because his wife Jean was expecting their fourth child. The Rams said, essentially, "Show up or get shipped out." When Wellington Mara heard Robustelli wanted to be closer to home, he swooped in, offering the Rams a first-round draft choice in exchange for the 6'1", 230-pound defensive end. It was the best trade the Giants ever made.

"Andy hits you so hard your bones rattle," Detroit Lions quarterback Bobby Layne once said of the man nicknamed "The Enforcer." Robustelli had such an impressive reputation that Mara once said the whole team whooped it up to celebrate the trade's announcement. "There has never been a reaction like that for a new player coming here. Not a draft pick like Lawrence Taylor. No one," Mara said.

In the next nine years, the Giants went to six championship games, winning in 1956; Robustelli, who scooped up twenty-two opponents' fumbles in his career, was named to five Pro Bowl teams and all-NFL teams in his years with the Giants and in 1962 became one of the few defensive players to be named the league's player of the year.

Robustelli, who was elected to the Hall of Fame in 1971, was smart and a leader—he was a player-coach in his final three seasons—but the first thing everyone who played with or coached Robustelli commented on was usually his work ethic.

"He put more book time into his work than the others," Tom Landry once said, after serving as the Giants' defensive coach from 1956 to 1959. "He thought all the time. Not just on the field, but in his room, at the dining table."

Robustelli shrugs compliments off—to him, working hard, all

the time, was just a way of life. "That's just what you do, you know," he says.

After Robustelli retired in 1964, he briefly returned to football in 1966, spending one year coaching the Brooklyn Dodgers of the upstart Continental Football League. (The team's general manager was none other than Jackie Robinson, but the club actually played most of its games on Randall's Island and was being sued by the Los Angeles Dodgers over the name when it folded after one season. The league collapsed not long after.)

But mostly he just kept working at the off-season job he had started while with the Rams when he had used his 1951 championship check to open a sports store. It had evolved into a sports marketing company that over time grew into Robustelli Corporate Services, which today offers everything from website and video production to sports marketing with a major emphasis on corporate travel and event planning.

It wasn't that this was Robustelli's dream job—he had already lived out his childhood fantasy. No, this was work. "You didn't necessarily pick something that was most likely to interest yourself, you picked something that would be of interest to people associated with you," he says. In other words, business executives would be thrilled to be associated with a superstar like Robustelli and would trust a player of Robustelli's caliber and integrity to be their guide through the world of sports, so it made sense for him to keep it going.

Robustelli says helping connect companies and athlete endorsers was very different in the days before the league expanded and before television became the powerhouse it is today. For starters, the dollars were a lot less. Also, the world was a lot smaller. "I knew a couple of people on each team so I could get an introduction to almost anyone," he says. Among those who worked with Robustelli's company back in the 1960s was a tight end for the Chicago Bears by the name of Mike Ditka.

The travel aspect came about almost by accident—Robustelli would arrange for a company to send a group of executives to visit an athlete or an event and gradually the company would begin to come to him to set up other travel services. As the world of business travel grew, so did his business. Then the international world opened up. That, of course, meant working hard to keep up. "As the business has progressed you have to make sure you stay on top of everything," Robustelli says.

Robustelli did take some time out in the 1970s to return to the Giants, serving as director of operations from 1974 through 1978. "The league was growing and the Maras were trying to restructure the team," he says. "I wasn't looking to get back into football but you'll always do it for your team, so I agreed to lend a hand if I could."

Robustelli originally thought he'd stay just a year or two, juggling his business and the Giants job, but found he couldn't. So he deputized others to run his business, although he'd always stop in on his way home to check up. But ultimately he left the Giants, feeling he had served his duty and needed to return to his business.

While Robustelli liked traveling when he was younger, one of the most appealing aspects of this job was setting up shop in Stamford to be close to his family. (His family also shares his love of sports—his son Rick played football at the University of Connecticut, and Rick's daughter Emily played softball at the University of Massachusetts). "It's the area I grew up in. My family is here," he says, adding that he even appreciates the cold New England winters. "I love the way the weather changes with the seasons."

These days, Robustelli doesn't even go to as many games as he used to, preferring the true home-field advantage. Yes, believe it or not, Andy Robustelli is finally taking it easy. "I'm almost retired," he says. "I just like to stay home and relax these days."

I n a Giants organization that has long prided itself on its sense of family, Sam Huff still can't quite fathom how he went so quickly from favored son to black sheep. After a lifetime filled with accomplishments and accolades, Huff knows he is a Giants legend, but he also knows that when Giants fans hear his name, many first think not of his on-field successes but of the ignominious trade that sent Huff to the Redskins and the Giants into the hinterlands, wandering for nearly two decades without a playoff appearance.

"When you were part of the Giants you were part of the family, and that's what hurt so bad," Huff says, still getting emotional four decades later. "It was like the family had kicked you out and they had never done that before."

Huff, now a Redskins radio announcer and founder of the West Virginia Breeders Classic horse race, says he still hugs Wellington Mara like a long-lost relative when they see each other, but some tension remains. "You can't undo what they let happen."

It was especially heartbreaking because Huff knew that Mara and the Giants had given him a life he hadn't even dared to dream about as a child in West Virginia. Born Robert Lee Huff in 1934 in the coal town of Edna Gas, Huff soon moved to a mining camp near Farmington—his family rented their house from the mining company and bought everything from a company store. Huff's father began working the mines at thirteen, his older brother at sixteen. From an early age, Huff knew he wanted to escape this dangerous and hardscrabble life, hoping that college could lead to a life as a football coach or teacher. Huff earned a football scholarship to West Virginia University (WVU), where he became an all-American, playing offensive guard and defensive tackle, helping lead the Mountaineers to their first ever top-ten ranking. (Huff, who in the 1980s was elected to both the College and Pro Football Halls of Fame, also played catcher on the WVU baseball team.)

The Giants picked the 6'1", 230-pound Huff in the third round—in the pros he'd be too small to continue playing offensive or defensive lineman, and his future was somewhat uncertain . . . until starting linebacker Ray Beck got hurt and Huff played well in his place. The defensive unit was gelling, and defensive coach Tom Landry implemented an innovative and aggressive 4-3 defense (one of the first ever), making Huff the middle linebacker and its heart and soul.

"It's like I was born to play linebacker," Huff says. "When I was up (instead of being a lineman) I could see everything."

Huff went on to win the Defensive Rookie of the Year award in 1956 as the Giants won the title. "That first year when I went into Yankee Stadium I felt like I was in the Hall of Fame," he recalls. "It was a special time to be athlete—I shared a locker with Mickey Mantle and got to know Mantle, Whitey Ford, and Yogi Berra."

With Landry calling plays that funneled traffic toward Huff while simultaneously giving Huff freedom to roam and induce mayhem, Huff became a perennial all-pro, leading the Giants back to the title game again and again. Huff became a national celebrity after Walter Cronkite hosted a CBS documentary called *The Violent World of Sam Huff*. He was also on the cover of *Time* magazine. Huff was the very face of Giants defense.

"I never let a back pass in front of me without clotheslining him," Huff has said of a then legal practice. "When I put that uniform on I was a completely different person. . . . I knocked my best friend (Joe Marconi of the Rams) . . . clear over the bench." Huff also once hit Green Bay running back Jimmy Taylor so hard his helmet dented.

And then, suddenly, it was over. In 1963, the Giants made it to the NFL championship for the sixth time in eight years, losing to the Chicago Bears 14–10 because of the offense's turnovers. But after the season Huff was traded to the Washington Redskins. "That trade was the biggest shock of my life," says Huff. "I still don't know for sure why it happened or why Wellington Mara let it happen."

Huff speculates that the offense-oriented Sherman hated that Huff led a defensive unit that shut down Sherman's offense in scrimmages and disliked the fact that the team's success was usually traced to a defense he had inherited from Tom Landry. The trade made the front pages in New York, and the Giants were subsequently taunted by their own fans yelling "Huff-Huff-Huff-Huff."

After that year the Giants collapsed, but Huff wanted his own personal vengeance. He got it two years later when his Redskins were trouncing the Giants 69–42. Rather than run up the score, Redskins coach Otto Graham was running out the clock, but Huff took charge with just seconds remaining and called a time-out and sent on the field goal unit to pile on another three points. (The seventy-two-point total remains the most the Giants have ever allowed.) "A linebacker is the one guy you don't want to get angry," Huff says, still relishing that moment. "It was a day of revenge. I wanted to get Sherman fired so badly."

While the trade to Washington stung Huff, it also opened up some very important doors. Huff had watched Giant teammate Kyle Rote moonlight as a broadcaster with his *Locker Room Report*, and, although he had never previously contemplated a career in broadcasting, when he went to Washington he began his own program from inside the Redskins clubhouse.

That led to a post-football career announcing radio. First he came back to the Giants, where he partnered with Marty Glickman, then in 1973 he returned to the Redskins, where he remains. "I think every athlete in broadcasting now owes a debt of gratitude to my teammates, Frank Gifford, Kyle Rote, and Pat Summerall, who led the way," says Huff, who also stayed on briefly after his playing days as an assistant coach under Vince Lombardi for the Redskins.

And in the 1980s, he would chat with Lawrence Taylor about the game's "wimps," complaining about quarterbacks that come out of the pocket but slide to avoid tackles: "They should have the guts to be hit like a man."

Some speculate that his delayed election to the Hall of Fame—six years after he became eligible—was due to the Cronkite documentary, believing that it glorified or exaggerated the game's violence, leading to the likes of Jack Tatum; others complained it gave Huff more credit than he deserved, with some even accusing him of being a pile-on artist. Huff has fought back by telling a story on himself about the time when defensive back Erich Barnes tackled Philadelphia running back Timmy Brown; when Brown yelled for Barnes to get off, according to Huff's story, Barnes said, "I can't get off until Huff gets here." Still, he takes his reputation seri-ously—when he learned he was finally elected to the Hall, he was quoted as saying, "I cried like a baby."

Today, Huff announces because he still loves the game and this keeps him a part of it, but just as he roamed far across the football field to make the play, he has ranged far in his life off the field.

During the 1960 presidential campaign, Huff had been asked by John Kennedy to introduce the aspiring candidate at a speech in West Virginia. It was a crucial moment for Kennedy because he was trying to overcome prejudice in Southern and rural states against the idea of a wealthy, Catholic president. In working-class, Protestant-heavy West Virginia, Huff's words carried weight. Ken-nedy won the primary, a turning point that knocked Hubert Hum-phrey from the race; Huff became friendly with Kennedy and his family. "Along with Tom Landry and Vince Lombardi, he was one of the three greatest men I ever knew," Huff says.

In 1970, his playing days behind him, Huff ran for Congress, challenging incumbent Robert Mollahan but losing in the West Vir-ginia Democratic primary.

But he was filled with ideas, other plans.

The very first time Huff had stayed at a Marriott hotel in New York he had been so impressed that he bought stock. Now he took a closer look at the hotel industry and saw that Marriott's hotels were half-empty every weekend, when businessmen were home with their families. Huff remembered how United Airlines had treated the Giants so well, using the same pilots and catering to their needs, that the Giants used United exclusively. So, he thought, why can't hotels also target sports—there are always teams and broadcasting crews traveling on weekends. He would be the guy who taught Marriott's staff how to attract the sports world.

Huff, of course, had no hotel experience. But Bill Marriott was a devoted Redskins fan, so he was certainly willing to meet with the famous Sam Huff. "I think he thought I was coming in to complain about something," Huff laughs. Huff persuaded Marriott to create sports reps in each hotel and to let Huff tackle the project. "They had to learn that if the Eagles are coming in to a Washington Marri-ott, you don't put up Redskins banners," he says, "and they had to learn that, say, George Allen wanted a milkshake in his room and Don Shula a six-pack of Budweiser."

Over the next twenty-seven years, Huff traveled the country for Marriott, using his knowledge of the sports world and the force of his own personality to make it all work. Each year, he'd hold a cookout for the NFL owners and general managers during the March owners' meetings, which kept Marriott in the good graces of the entire league. But in 1989, during tough times for the hotel business, a superior told him that there'd be no budget for the annual feast. "I said, 'You can't treat me like I'm one of your sales-people. You don't want to make me angry or I'll put your ass through that wall,'" Huff says. "That's just the way I am." The boss, not surprisingly, backed down.

These days Huff devotes his time and energy to a bunch of ath-letes who would never stay at a hotel—racehorses. Huff traces his interest in horses to his days with the Giants, when he and his teammates all mingled at Toots Shor's not only with baseball play-ers but also with the top jockeys. "I used to go to Aqueduct to see them race," Huff says. Then, during his Marriott days, he dealt with horse people during the Kentucky Derby and other big events. Eventually he began buying up racehorses; after a divorce he built a twenty-three-acre horse farm for breeding and raising horses in Middleburg, West Virginia.

"It's the only sport where you don't need so many millions to be an owner," he says. "And it's exciting as hell, it really is."

In the 1980s, when Huff learned that the Charles Town Racetrack was endangered, he used his fame and political skill to help per-suade state legislators to vote to allow a percentage of state-run slot machine money to help preserve the track by subsidizing a new race Huff launched called the West Virginia Breeders' Cup. Patterned after the Maryland Million and run each October, the Breeders' Cup has become the richest and most prestigious race in the state, attracting major sponsors and even coverage by ESPN.

Through his interest in horses, Huff also met Carol Holden. To-gether they founded the Middleburg Broadcasting Network, which produces a regional weekly radio show on racing called *Trackside* that the two—now a couple—host together. "She won't let me talk about football on there, but I slip it in," he says.

For Huff, that's only fitting. After all, he's a guy who still has a picture of his dad in his mining uniform in his office, a reminder of where he came from. But in addition to coming from the mines of West Virginia, Huff, of course, also came to the world from football, specifically from the golden era of the New York Giants.

Dick Modzelewski learned about playing football from his dad. Joseph Modzelewski never actually played the game—he was a Polish immigrant who toiled for thirty-three years in the coal mines near the family's home in West Natrona, Pennsylvania, thirty miles east of Pittsburgh. But he passed his work ethic and attitude on to his son, who would go on to NFL greatness with the legendary Giants teams of the late 1950s and who would set a league record by playing in 180 consecutive games.

"I was aware of the record and was proud of it," Modzelewski says. (The record was later broken by Minnesota's Jim Marshall.) "I was a lunch-bucket kind of guy—I'd come to work and do my job. I always pictured myself as my dad, spending all those years in the coal mines, working hard and never complaining."

Modzelewski says the tunnel coal mines were a half-mile outside of town, while in town "there were steel factories all around us." In summers, he'd work at the Allegheny-Ludlum Steel Company or, one year, at a chemical company that made DDT. "It was tough," he says, adding that his brother Ed—who would go on to stardom ahead of Dick both at the University of Maryland and in the NFL—even spent one summer in those coal tunnels, vowing never to go back again. (Ed's forceful presence earned him the nickname "Big Mo," which left only "Little Mo" for Dick, even though he eventually outgrew "Big Mo," reaching 6' tall and 260 pounds; their younger brother, Eugene, who played college football at New Mexico State, got stuck with "No Mo.")

In high school, Modzelewski played both offense and defense like everyone else, but from the beginning he always thought of himself as a defensive player. "To be honest with you, I was kind of a half-assed offensive player," he says.

He was named all-state and recruited by Notre Dame, the University of South Carolina, and others, but he chose Maryland, in part because he was impressed by coach Jim Tatum and in part because Ed was already there, playing fullback. There, Big and Lit-

tle Mo helped lead Maryland to a national title, with Little Mo playing three years as starter and, in his senior year, earning all-American status and the Outland Trophy for best inside lineman.

The Washington Redskins drafted Modzelewski in the second round, but he nearly spurned them when their initial offer was absurdly low. "They came to my room at Maryland to make the offer, for $3,200," he recalls. His brother had received a $10,000 salary and $3,000 bonus the previous year from the hometown Steelers, although he played an admittedly more glamorous position. What Modzelewski found particularly galling was that his offer was far below the $6,200 his father was earning laboring in the coal mine.

Ultimately, he pressured owner George Preston Marshall into signing him for $6,500, with a $1,500 bonus, but their relations remained bumpy. Although Modzelewski became a starter as a rookie, by the end of his sophomore season he was ready to jump to the Canadian Football League, where the Calgary Stampeders were willing to pay him far more money. But Marshall sued his own player, and the Canadians told Modzelewski that he'd be sidelined while the case worked its way through the courts. Still, the defensive lineman refused to return to Washington and told Marshall to trade him.

Marshall traded him to Pittsburgh, briefly uniting Little Mo with Big Mo, but the Steelers experience soon proved more unpleasant than life in Washington. The problem was coach Walt Kiesling, "a horrible coach," Modzelewski says. "It was the worst year I ever spent in football, even though it was in my hometown."

Kiesling forced Big Mo to play through a back injury in training camp, then grew angry and packed him off to Cleveland (where Paul Brown let him rest in a hospital till he was well enough to return and help the team win the NFL championship). Later Kiesling fined Little Mo for going home to be with his wife when their first baby was born, although team owner Art Rooney eventually talked Kiesling into forgetting the fine.

(Kiesling is also known for cutting a scrawny young Pennsylvania boy trying out for quarterback, but Modzelewski actually agreed with Kiesling's assessment—when the Calgary coach called looking for quarterbacks who might be available, Little Mo said, "They might cut this skinny-ass kid named Unitas, but I wouldn't even bother with him"; later, when he saw John Unitas, shoulders hunched forward in the rain, on his way to Baltimore for a tryout, Modzelewski told his wife, "He'll never make it.")

Modzelewski refused to return, telling the Steelers' front office he wanted them to "pay me a million dollars or trade me." The team arranged a three-way deal with the Detroit Lions and New York that ended up shipping the disgruntled player to the Giants. There, he finally found a home.

He was a Giant from 1956 to 1963, the exact span of the glory years as the team went 723-25-4, won one championship, and reached the big game five more times.

Modzelewski arrived the same year as Andy Robustelli, but the two newcomers clicked immediately with the rest of the defensive unit. "We all became friends, family even—we immediately played as a team," he says. "I believe that all stemmed from the Mara family, from the way they were, family-wise. I tried coaching that way later on and it worked for a while, although later on I couldn't get it done as the players and game changed."

Even when success—the championship and the attention it bestowed on them—soon followed, Modzelewski said there was no jealousy or rivalry among teammates. "When Sam Huff was on the cover of *Time* magazine we were all proud of him," he says. "We were totally one."

After the 1963 season, however, they were ripped apart by coach Allie Sherman. The brothers Modzelewski were living in Cleveland, where they ran a restaurant called Mo and Junior's Restaurant; soon after the Giants lost the 1963 championship game, Huff, who was visiting the restaurant, went to Little Mo's office to field a phone call. "When he came down, I said, 'You look terrible,' and he said, 'I've just been traded.' Two weeks later I got the same call."

At least Modzelewski was shipped out to the Browns, which was for the best because he had his family, home, and restaurant there and because they were a top-flight team—he'd win another NFL championship that next season. But that didn't ease the pain of being torn away from what he considered his family. "I was hurt very badly. I was angry," he says, recalling a photograph of him and Huff walking off the field together in their new uniforms after a Browns-Redskins game looking up at the scoreboard that showed the Giants were going down in defeat.

Although it especially upset him that "no one has ever sat down with me and said 'This is why we traded you,'" Modzelewski remains loyal to the team that brought him his greatest moments of joy and accomplishment. "To this day I always say I'm a Giant."

Modzelewski played three seasons with Cleveland, but after 1966 he remembered that Charley Conerly had once told him "it was time to quit if you still felt sore on the day of the next game. I was sore." And so he was done.

He was not done with football, however. While his restaurant business would last sixteen years and he and his brother also operated a thirteen-shop chain of roast beef fast food outlets and even briefly a farm with Hereford cattle ("I enjoyed the work although there was not much money in that"), he stayed in the game until 1989. Right after retiring he spent weekends scouting for Cleveland but soon had offers from the Browns, Steelers, and 49ers about coaching. He chose Cleveland, returning as a defensive line coach—he worked for the next twenty-two years as line coach and defensive coordinator for the Browns, Cincinnati Bengals, and Detroit Lions. (Of course, back then, when staffs were smaller, Modzelewski did double duty as defensive coordinator and defensive line coach simultaneously.) As a coach, Modzelewski viewed himself less as a drill sergeant and more as a teacher. "I believe you should be a good enough coach to make any player better than when you got him," he says, adding that "even on my last day of coaching with the Lions I was still studying the game."

These days, Little Mo lives the quiet retired life in New Bern, North Carolina, where he likes to go fishing when he's not on a road trip to Atlanta, Cleveland, or Chicago to visit his children and grandchildren. Of course, he only hits the road "between operations," since he has needed a new knee, two back operations, and two shoulder operations, the price he paid for being a guy who didn't miss a game in nearly thirteen years. But to him, the cost is minimal compared to everything he's gotten from his life in football, especially with the Giants. "Would I do it all again? Absolutely, yes."

Harland Svare is a man with a mission. He wants to change the way America gets in shape, and he has just the plan to make it happen. He calls it the Svare Sports Training Method.

Of course, the former linebacker has long been a man on the move, always pushing up against the cutting edge. Svare, the son of a butter maker in Minnesota, graduated from Washington State and was drafted in 1953 by the Los Angeles Rams. The former end quickly became one of the first crop of outside linebackers in the NFL's evolving defensive schemes. Two years later he was traded to the Giants, for whom he played during the glory years in the late 1950s.

As his career was winding down, the Giants briefly tried Svare as a player-coach, having him replace Landry as defensive coordinator in 1960. When the team let him go as both player and coach, he returned to the Rams, where he briefly served as defensive line coach before becoming the youngest head coach in football history at age thirty-one halfway through the 1962 season.

Coaching wasn't something Svare had planned on, but despite his youth, he says, "I had an advantage"—referring to the years he spent studying the game at the feet of the Giants' legendary coaching staff led by Jimmie Lee Howell and a couple of assistants named Tom Landry and Vince Lombardi.

But the upbeat and straightforward Svare was coaching a young team and later admitted that while he had the football knowledge, he probably didn't have the maturity to be a head coach at that point.

The Rams went 0-5-1 for the rest of 1962 and were 14-31-3 overall before he lost his job after three and a half years—just as it was all coming together, especially the Fearsome Foursome Rams defense he helped create. (The Rams would finish 8-6 in 1966 without him and then win their division the following year.) He then returned to the Giants as a defensive coordinator in 1967 and 1968 before joining Lombardi in Washington. After Lombardi died, Svare was on the move again, this time taking over as both general manager and head coach for the San Diego Chargers. It was not a match made in heaven.

"I didn't like being a GM," he says. "I didn't like negotiating all day long with agents. That wasn't me. That wasn't fun."

The coaching soon ceased being fun as Svare inadvertently plunged into a controversy that would plague the NFL for years afterward. He was concerned about the Chargers' inconsistency. He hired a psychiatrist to look into the team's issue, but peering beneath the surface revealed discomfiting information about growing drug use—both amphetamines and marijuana—by players who were smuggling stuff in from Mexico.

"I had some suspicions and tried to stop it," he says. The revelations infuriated everyone from fans to NFL commissioner Pete Rozelle, and Svare resigned as coach in 1973, although he stayed for several more years as general manager. And today, he points out that if the league had pushed aggressively then it could have headed off some of the drug trouble and steroid problems that subsequently cropped up. (Svare also says Rozelle later apologized and refunded him a fine related to the whole mess.)

As a coach, he also flopped on the field, going 7-17 over parts of three seasons. He is most remembered for his belief that Oakland Raiders owner Al Davis was spying on his team's pregame meetings. In an oft-quoted story, Svare looked up at a lightbulb in the locker room and yelled, "Damn you, Al Davis, I know you're listening." (Davis later remarked that there was nothing in the lightbulb, but he said it in a way that implied there was a bug elsewhere in the room.)

Svare would have returned to coaching but felt he was persona non grata after the Chargers affair. "After that I did a lot of different things but I never really had my heart in any of them," he says. It took a leg infection to get his heart racing again.

In 1981 Svare suffered a knee infection that got so bad he needed surgery . . . again and again. After six operations over the next few years Svare was virtually crippled, unable to go up or down stairs. He seemed headed for an artificial knee. Then one day his wife Annette (a former Giants secretary) tried an alternative therapy for a back problem. When she recovered quickly, Svare went to her healer, Pete Egoscue, and said, "Heal me."

Egoscue was an ex-Marine who rehabbed his own hamstring after a bullet wound in Vietnam and developed a unique but commonsense approach to treating injuries that focused heavily on fixing the body's alignment and stopping one part of the body from compensating for problems in another part to create a full range of motion. With Svare he focused not on the knee but on the hip flexor—the ex-Giant was swinging his whole leg instead of flexing the hip—and soon enough, Svare was pain free and then able to run again.

Svare was so amazed that he became Egoscue's partner, helping him in the struggle to gain credibility for a man with no medical background. The Egoscue method gained ground after Jack Nicklaus testified that Egoscue's exercises saved his golfing career. Svare and Egoscue then opened clinics in Del Mar, California, and Palm Beach, Florida.

Svare, who today lives in the San Diego suburb of Carlsbad, began applying Egoscue's ideas to training instead of therapy and, after spending the better part of a decade working with Egoscue, went off on his own to focus on this proactive approach.

He has even created a training course called The Patch that has been used by the University of Washington and several California high schools. The exercises promote proper alignment to maximize the flow of oxygen throughout the body but also use every part of the body so that "you're moving while you're moving," Svare explains, adding that unlike many trainers he wants to develop the fast- and slow-twitch muscles together, not in isolation.

"I'm on a mission now," he says. It is a mission with numerous obstacles, however. For starters, he says, children today spend too much time in cars, lugging heavy backpacks, or sitting in front of televisions and computers. "They don't develop their bodies," he says, adding that the overemphasis on weight training among athletes actually compounds problems instead of helping because without other training it can cause posture and alignment problems. "I want people to be 'farm boy strong.' I was a farm boy and you used your body in all kinds of ways as you grew up."

Budget cuts in the California school system have slowed him down, as has the skepticism that faces anything new. "People are just not open-minded about new things," Svare says. "This hasn't taken off yet."

Still, Svare, who still pushes himself on a daily basis, running steps on the beaches near his home, remains determined. "I'm working very hard getting the word out," he says, adding that he wants to bring his methods not only to schoolchildren and competitive athletes but also to retired NFL players who played injured and now find themselves struggling to overcome a lifetime of compensation and bad habits. "I really want to get them going," says Svare.

When Roosevelt "Rosey" Grier was growing up in rural Georgia, he knew next to nothing about organized football. "When we played football it was just a bunch of kids and they'd throw a ball up in the air and beat up on whoever caught it," he recalls fondly and with a chuckle.

But in a way that was perfect training for the NFL and for life— the rough-and-tumble, stop-the-ball-carrier-at-all-costs approach certainly seems appropriate training for one of the best defensive linemen of his generation, and the go-with-the-flow improvised quality of the game perfectly sums up the life that was in store for him, full of surprises and adventures, virtually all of it unstructured and unplanned.

"My life is just like this: it just happens," says Grier, an all-pro who actually played more seasons with the Giants (seven) than with the Los Angeles Rams (four), but who was overshadowed by the likes of Sam Huff and Andy Robustelli in New York and who is best remembered for his days in LA as the leader of the Fearsome Foursome. "I look at myself spending a weekend at the White House with Jimmy Carter or having lunch on Air Force One with Ronald Reagan and Frank Sinatra and say, 'What in the world am I doing here?' It always amazes me."

Of course, what amazes the 6'6", 300-pound star is not so much his ascension from sandlot football to the NFL as it is his continued evolution to recording star, actor, footnote to political history, author, needlepoint celebrity, grassroots activist, and minister. It's been a busy and largely fulfilling life for a larger-than-life peanut farmer's son.

Named for Franklin Delano Roosevelt, Grier was the seventh of eleven children, a trait that taught him another valuable lesson— the importance of getting along with those around you. On the Giants he would always be one who strived for team harmony, to bring people together; in his preaching in recent decades, he'd often work with white ministers to break down the segregation that plagues America's churches.

Grier lived on the farm till he was eleven, when his family moved north to Rosedale, New Jersey, after his father got a job at Allied Chemical. It was a move that changed his life.

"I was so happy. In Georgia I had to beg to go to school: 'Poppa, can I go to school today?' and he'd say, 'Not today, son, we have too much work to do.' But in New Jersey they made you go to school."

Grier didn't know much about football or basketball, but the coaches saw how big he was and invited him out to play both sports. "On my first day for football I put my glasses and books down and went to go get a uniform, but I put them down on the field and when I came back they had played over my stuff and my glasses were broken," Grier recalls, adding that he had trouble in basketball because he could not catch the ball very well. But with football, Grier soon taught himself to play the line well—very well, in fact.

"I used to watch small guys and how quickly they could get off when the play started and I decided that I was big but if I could get off like them I'd be effective," he says. "It changed my life."

But it wasn't football that landed Grier a scholarship at Penn State, it was track: he was an all-American star in shot put, discus, and relay. Grier didn't think about professional football until his senior year of college when teams started sending out questionnaires. "I sent them all back and said, 'No, I only want to play for the Giants,'" he says. "Those were my negotiating skills."

He went in the third round, to the Los Angles Rams. The Giants, who had traded for Los Angeles's third-round pick, snatched Grier. He played in 1955 and then for the 1956 championship team before missing a season to serve in the Army at Fort Ord. He was back with the Giants for the fabled 1958 season, along with the championship games of 1959, 1961, and 1962.

"That team had great leaders," he says. But what truly amazed him was the racial harmony—he expected that a team coached by Jim Lee Howell of Arkansas and featuring stars like Charley Conerly from Mississippi would be an uncomfortable and intimidating place to be. "But Jim Lee Howell was always fair and I got to be good friends with Charley. My precept was nothing like what they were."

During the off-season, Grier would earn more money off the

field than he did as a Giant by traveling with rock bands, emceeing and occasionally singing. But his recording career got started because of Kyle Rote.

"Kyle Rote got me into singing professionally," he says, explaining that when he came back from his stint in the Army he carried his guitar with him everywhere. "I'd keep everyone on the team up at night with my playing."

But Rote thought he was talented and put him in touch with producers and a voice coach. Most of his records were on small labels and failed to crack the charts, but nevertheless he loved writing and performing music, in places as prestigious as Carnegie Hall. He wrote about twenty songs and recorded twenty-five records overall. He recorded songs like "Moonlight in Vermont," "In My Tenement," originals like "Slow Drag," and remakes of classics like "Spanish Harlem." He even did a football-related song called "Who's Got the Ball (Y'all)." His 1968 single "People Make the World" at least cracked the Billboard Singles Chart at #126.

Grier loved his days with the Giants and especially loved his teammates, but although he spent nearly two-thirds of his career in New York, he embraces the popular identity of himself as a Ram. "That's the city that traded for me, so I'll go with the Rams," he says, recalling the trade that "really, really broke my heart."

Grier was the first of the Giants' defensive stars to be inexplicably traded by Allie Sherman, who later infamously packed off Dick Modzelewski and Sam Huff. Grier heard a rumor from an interviewer in Connecticut in 1962, then later mentioned on TV that he'd heard he was going to be traded. Wellington Mara responded to fan outrage by personally calling Grier to tell him he was staying put, but soon after, Sherman called to tell him he was gone. "I wasn't angry, but I was really disappointed—I'd sacrificed myself for that team and fought for those players," he says. "I thought for a second about not playing anymore but I was a football player and I was a professional."

It helped that former teammate Harland Svare was running the show out in Los Angeles and had several other ex-Giants on board. What helped even more was teaming up with Deacon Jones, Merlin Olson, and Lamar Lundy to create the Fearsome Foursome, the league's most dominant defensive line. Grier came in with enormous credibility, having played for a perennial winner, although it took his macho teammates a while to appreciate his answer to their question about why the Giants won: "Because we loved each other." The Rams never found the winning way during Grier's four years there, failing to reach the playoffs each time.

And Grier never made it out for the 1967 season—the year the Rams went 11-1—his career was ended suddenly by a torn Achilles tendon. Grier, of course, was never at a loss for something new to do. He even took up needlepoint.

In 1970, Grier, who was divorced, was driving in Beverly Hills when "I saw these ladies going in a store, and I mean beautiful ladies." Entranced, he parked his car, slung his guitar over his back, and followed them in, determined to work his charm. It was a shop for needlepoint and other crafts. Grier tried chatting them up but, of course, was talking about something he knew nothing about. "So someone there said, 'Rosey, if you're going to talk to the women you have to know what they're talking about.'"

So Grier started learning needlepoint. One day, they asked him to pose for photos with some of the women, and soon his picture was in the paper. That led to a book offer, which he turned down but later agreed to, producing *Rosey Grier's Needlepoint for Men* in 1973; he also ended up with a centerfold spread of him doing needlepoint in *Look* magazine. That led to an invitation from actress Marlo Thomas to join the cast of *Free to Be . . . You and Me*, in which he sang the poignant song "It's All Right to Cry."

"I proved you could still be a man and sew and then I got to be the guy that people would use to tell kids that it was okay to show feelings," Grier says proudly.

Meanwhile, in 1967, he had been invited to Washington by Ethel Kennedy for a fundraiser for a program that brought urban children to the country. When Ethel and Bobby Kennedy met Grier at their door, Kennedy playfully hit Grier and took off, with the defensive lineman in pursuit. "We hit it off right away," Grier says, adding that he was up till late that night mingling with everyone from Supreme Court Justice "Whizzer" White to the singing duo Peaches and Herb.

"What I really liked about Bobby and Ethel was the way they treated people—it had nothing to do with color or status, everyone was the same. I've always tried to do that."

Grier adds that he had never been involved in politics before meeting Kennedy, who inspired him, like so many others, to take an interest in public and community life. Grier also became active in the Kennedy family's Special Olympics program (although that bond ended in the 1980s when Grier, who had become an ordained minister, turned Republican).

After that, the Kennedys and Grier would get together in Washington and Los Angeles, and when Kennedy began running for president, Grier volunteered his services. Kennedy would have him sing "Spanish Harlem" at his rallies or even speak when Kennedy couldn't make it; on other occasions, Grier would act as extra security, helping out bodyguard Bill Barry.

Security was Grier's role on the fateful night of the California primary, when Kennedy said near the end of his speech, "Rosey Grier said he would take care of anybody who didn't vote for me." Moments later, Kennedy was dead, and Grier would forever be linked to that night in the public's collective mind.

"I was assigned to Ethel Kennedy and Bobby was supposed to come to me after his speech, but he jumped off the back of the stage and went another way," Grier says. "We followed and we were moving through the cameramen and I was trying to protect Ethel. Then I heard the shots. I went down with Ethel then I came up running. I saw people struggling but they didn't have control of the guy. I grabbed his legs and pulled him up on a table. George Plimpton was struggling with the gun hand but the gun was waving at his face. I put my thumb under the hammer and wrestled it out and put it in my pocket."

Grier says he later gave the gun to Olympic star Rafer Johnson, another Kennedy friend who had also helped in the chaos, and Johnson turned the gun over to police. In recent years, however, Johnson has publicly claimed he is the one who took the gun away from Sirhan Sirhan, a claim Grier vigorously disputes. "That's not the truth; he changed his story. My story has never changed," Grier says.

Grier was also one of the men there who helped prevent the gathering crowd from attacking and possibly killing Kennedy's assassin. In the aftermath of the assassination, Grier was despondent. He would soon turn full-time to acting, a career that served him well for a while before leaving him disillusioned.

He certainly didn't miss football, since he was making more

money and learning to express himself. Acting was, like singing, a liberating experience. "I used to be afraid to talk," Grier says. "When I was in high school in New Jersey I had a Georgia accent and I wasn't very well versed in the English language. Acting drew me out."

Grier was a regular on *Daniel Boone* in its last season, playing runaway slave Gabe Cooper. He then appeared in everything from the low-budget *The Thing with Two Heads*, in which his head was on the same body as a racist scientist played by Ray Milland, to *Roots: The Next Generation*. Along the way, he appeared on countless talk shows as well as classic 1970s series like *Love Boat*, *Kojak*, *The Jeffersons*, *ChiPs*, and *The White Shadow*. But most of his movie roles were in films like *Rabbit Test* and *Evil in the Deep*, and he gradually grew disillusioned with acting, and with his life in general.

"I had a lot of opportunities, but after a while it seemed like a charade," he says. "The acting and the money and the fame weren't enough for me. There had to be something better."

Grier had been trying to help gang kids, but he was doing it in a fairly haphazard way, taking them to a Rams practice or to meet celebrities or giving speeches. But then he realized "I needed help and I was as lost as they were." So Grier began searching and, inspired by his young son, ended up rediscovering religion. He soon remarried his second wife, whom he had also divorced, dedicating himself to his family, his religion, and public service.

He became an ordained minister in 1983 and helped raise money for a California group called Giant Step, which built housing for senior citizens and trained teens for jobs; he also worked with the Foundations of the Milken Families (as in Michael Milken, the former Wall Street hotshot who went to jail), which has enabled him to use their name to accomplish his goals for helping inner-city children. Grier even went and ministered to O. J. Simpson when the troubled former football star was facing murder charges— Grier got considerable grief for that outreach but did it because he saw Simpson being left alone by other men of faith.

But Grier's biggest and most ambitious projects, first Are You Committed and now Impact Urban America, are grassroots programs he has started himself. Are You Committed was started in the 1980s to provide educational and spiritual programs for youths while finding them jobs to connect them to society. Impact Urban America has a larger scope, aiming to bring churches and the corporate world together to serve poor people—the churches can help the inner self while the corporations can provide more pragmatic training.

All these efforts to help people grow and find themselves make perfect sense for Grier, since the man of a thousand lives says he's still growing and changing. "I still don't think I'm all grown up yet," he says. "But with all this time comes wisdom and understanding, and if we have the energy and the power there are lots of things we can do to help ourselves and improve the lives of others."

service, he decided to go ahead and play for the Redskins. Then, since the Army had heard him publicly complain that he was "stuck" for two years, they let him go almost immediately. And then Lynch got another break—he was unhappy in Washington, but he was also on the most-wanted list of the Giants' savvy defensive coordinator Tom Landry, and in the spring of 1959 the team sent Washington a fourth draft choice for Lynch.

The 6'2", 195-pound cornerback made himself right at home in New York, leading the league with nine interceptions in 1961 and 1963 (when he was invited to the Pro Bowl); he also led the team in pickoffs in 1964 and 1965. And in 1964 he moved with his family to Douglaston, Queens, where he still lives. "It's the best spot in New York City," he says.

When Lynch first came to the Giants, the team was a powerhouse, and he helped them return to the NFL championship game for three straight years beginning in 1961. Soon after, the team fell on hard times, and Lynch was nearing the end of his career when a single play hurried him out of the game. In 1966 in a game against the Steelers, he went to knock a player out of bounds and ended up on the ground paralyzed and terrified, flashing on Roy Campanella's accident that left him paralyzed. It took almost fifteen minutes for sensation to return to his body. "It was a real eye-opener," he says. Although he didn't quit right then, it inspired his wife Roz, a former Miss Pennsylvania with a strong backbone, to get him thinking about retiring. "I know I did the right thing." She had also been the one who told him football was only a game and she would only marry him if he got a real job in the off-season. Coach Allie Sherman soon got him a sales job for a printing company named Shorewood Press.

Lynch had no interest in coaching and rejected an offer from Tim Mara to do radio broadcasting, so he made his off-season sales job a full-time gig. In the late 1960s he got involved as part owner (along with former New York Giant Pat Summerall and former New York Yankee Whitey Ford) of Transnational Communications, a company that owned radio stations and pro teams including the NHL's Oakland Seals.

The company soon went bankrupt, but it served a pivotal role in Lynch's life—he began doing radio broadcasts of Giants games for his stations. Afterward, when Sam Huff left the Giants broadcast

I n the end, the football games—even the big ones, the NFL title games or the Pro Bowl games—mattered less than you might think. Ask the perennial Giant Dick Lynch about the highlights of his career and he doesn't mention any big games or big plays, not even the record-setting three interceptions he returned for touchdowns in 1963 or the bone-jarring hit on Billy Wade in that year's championship against the Chicago Bears that caused a fumble, leading to the team's first touchdown.

No, what Lynch savors from his playing days is the esprit de corps, especially among the defense, which thought of itself as a unit, not eleven individuals. Their camaraderie didn't end on the playing field either—after the games Lynch would meet up again with players like Andy Robustelli, Sam Huff, or Kyle Rote, and even sometimes owner Wellington Mara, at favorite hangouts like Gallagher's or P. J. Clarke's or Toots Shor's. For Lynch, that's what it was all about, "a great group of guys. We're still pals to thi' day." Indeed, the veteran Giants radio broadcaster talks with hi' ex-teammates on the phone and visits with them on the road. Ar he knows that if he needs them, they'll be there for him, as th were when tragedy struck Lynch's family in 2001.

Lynch, born in 1936, grew up as a Giants fan in the Great N area of Long Island and then in Patenburg, New Jersey, wher' lived on a farm. He then starred at Notre Dame as a running l and defensive back. He was most noted for his offense, leadin' team in pass receptions (thirteen catches for 128 yards) in his s year, and when Notre Dame snapped Oklahoma's record-s forty-seven-game winning streak on the Sooners' home turf, Lynch who broke the 0–0 tie in the fourth quarter, scorin pitchout.

Lynch was drafted by the Washington Redskins in 1958 on the verge of instead taking a job with Encyclopaedia Br in Chicago; however, Lynch had joined the ROTC in col suddenly found himself drafted for two years. Since he take the job he wanted and had time to kill before rep booth, he agreed to become the official color analyst for the Giants, a job he still has three decades later. "I never thought I'd be doing it this long, but it was the best thing that ever happened to me," he says. "Announcing keeps me right in the game, watching practices, talking to the players, understanding how the game has changed."

But Lynch was as aggressive off the field as on it, and he soon took another job on top of his radio work, as a broker for government bonds, eventually becoming president of Tri-State Capital Markets Group; Lynch even managed to mesh his two worlds by wining and dining customers in every city the Giants visited each season, giving those clients an extra thrill by bringing them to meet the players.

Lynch gave up contact sports after that one hit, but he never stopped moving. When he quit, the Giants' team doctor urged him to take up jogging. Lynch was initially aghast at the thought of pushing himself more physically. "I said, 'That's why I'm quitting' . . . but it really woke me up." While many ex-jocks "eat and get fat," Lynch ran with a passion, starting by running in Central Park and building up to the point where he even ran a marathon on Long Island.

And while Douglaston is more a tennis hotbed than a football one, Lynch fit in fine. He was an avid tennis player for years, becoming friends with the McEnroes and playing tennis with Mary Carillo's father, Tony, while several of his children earned tennis scholarships for college.

On some levels, Lynch is showing his age—he has given up the government bond job ("it's a young man's game") and he no longer plays tennis ("I have two new hips, another thing I got from football")—but in reality, he's still going strong. He is still at his playing weight of 195 pounds. He still plays golf regularly, especially at former teammate Tommy Costello's Great Rock Golf Course in Long Island, and he still runs—even in the dead of winter he'll go twelve miles to the Throgs Neck Bridge and back. (He does admit to pushing himself a bit less, walking part of the way these days, saying, "I'm not going to the Olympics . . . I just discovered that.")

For years, Lynch led a charmed life—a beautiful wife, six children, and a close-knit family, success and recognition on and off the football field. But everything changed on September 11, 2001.

His son Richie, who had followed Lynch into the government bond business, worked in the Twin Towers and was killed in the terrorist attacks that day, leaving behind a wife, Christina, and a young daughter, Olivia. "It was a horrible experience," Lynch says, his voice growing thick. "We still haven't gotten over it. We won't."

Lynch still feels the spirit of his son with him, even while he's announcing at games. "He's there as far as I'm concerned," he says. Lynch was thankful to have football to go back to, "to be able to keep doing what I was doing," but he didn't simply lose himself in his work. He also did what he could to help out. At home, of course, that meant frequent visits with Olivia. ("She'll be a Lynch, no doubt about it.") But Lynch had already been involved in various charities, especially through the NFL Alumni group, and now he devoted his energy to this cause, working with the NFL's relief fund and with Tuesday's Children, a group that raises money for children who lost a parent on 9/11.

Then he went and started his own fundraiser, the Richard and Olivia Lynch Tournament, at Costello's golf club. He got plenty of support from various friends including John McEnroe, but what moved him most of all was how his former teammates rallied to his side. "They know when to come together," he says, rattling off the names of buddies who have shown up for the tournaments: Frank Gifford, Alex Webster, Rosey Brown—even a very ill Kyle Rote came to the first one, carting machinery to help him breathe. (Rote died soon after.)

It's that bond that makes Lynch glad he played for this team. When he says he "played with the real Giants," he's referring not just to the team's name but to the stature of his teammates.

Once, long ago, there was no stopping Cliff Livingston. The Giants linebacker was a major presence on the field during the team's glory days and off the field as well, where he made the most of the New York nightlife. And unlike so many football players, Livingston managed to escape the debilitating injuries that take their toll later in life, leaving retired players hobbling and in pain. That's why the past few years have been so frustrating for the hardworking Californian, who has been sidelined by a painful injury that happened a lifetime away from the football field.

"I'm a workaholic and a very physical person, so the past few years have been tough," says Livingston, explaining that he required back surgery in 2001 after he slipped while helping a plumber move a 100-gallon water heater while on the job at his building maintenance business.

Still, when Livingston looks back at the big picture, he knows how fortunate he has been, recalling that when he started playing in the NFL the average career was only three years and the average life span was only sixty for an NFL player—Livingston, who played from 1954 until 1965, far surpassed all expectations while living the good life in New York.

Livingston's path to New York was not a traditional one. He grew up in the town of Montebello in Southern California. Back in the 1940s, professional football ranked fairly low on the national sports radar—far beneath baseball, boxing, and college football—but not in the Livingston household.

"I was indoctrinated into professional football because my brother Howie was playing and getting paid $1,800 a year," remembers Livingston, whose top salary two decades later was $21,000 in 1963. (Howie played for nine NFL seasons, including four years for the Giants, from 1944 to 1947; he missed two years during the Korean War and came back for one more year in 1953, the year before Cliff turned pro.) "That's where my excitement came from. I couldn't believe he was getting paid to play football."

In high school and at a junior college called Orange Coast College, Livingston played football and a little baseball and was a track star. "I wanted to become another Bob Mathias. I even did a couple of decathlons in junior college." (Although the javelin and shot and other track events have little direct connection to playing defense in the NFL, Livingston is convinced that the track events helped his game, improving his coordination and strength.)

Livingston then transferred to UCLA, where he majored in physical education—"it was the easiest thing I could get through"—before being drafted by the military and spending twenty-one months at Fort Ord on the Monterey Peninsula. (He was let out three months early because the Korean War had already ended and he was to report for practice with the Giants that summer.)

Serving in the military helped prepare Livingston for life in the NFL, since his Fort Ord team (and its opponents) featured numerous established NFL players (including Ollie Matson, Ed Henke, and Stan Campbell) as well as other future NFL players (including future Giants Don Heinrich and Dave Mann, plus Bud Roffler, Burt Delavan, and Earl Putnam)—all told, twenty-one of the forty players would end up in the NFL.

"That really whetted my appetite for playing professional football," Livingston says, adding that by the time he arrived in the NFL he knew he could compete at that level.

The team lost exhibition games to the Los Angeles Rams and San Francisco 49ers but won thirteen straight against military foes, outscoring opponents by a stunning 524–74. The players gained attention by trouncing Quantico for the All-Service Championship in the Poinsettia Bowl 55–19, then beat the Great Lakes Naval Training Center team 67–12 in the Salad Bowl (which became the Fiesta Bowl). Still, Livingston says family ties are what led to the Giants' signing him as a free agent. "The only reason the Giants ever looked at me was that Jim Lee Howell had played football with my brother Howie," he says.

The Giants signed him to be a defensive lineman since football was dominated in those days by the 7-4 defense, but not long after his arrival, assistant coach Tom Landry instituted his famed 4-3 defense and Livingston moved to linebacker.

"I loved playing in New York," he says, adding that he probably saw every play on and off Broadway during his years with the Giants, getting to know all the backstage personnel. But while he limited his drinking somewhat during the season, his nightlife was about more than just the theater. "I lived downtown because that's where all the action was," he says. "I pushed the envelope, trust me. I probably did a lot of things that people hadn't even thought of."

For instance, there was the time that he was really being bothered by the fluttering of a pigeon outside the window of the hotel room he lived in during the season. So Livingston grabbed his bow and arrow and fired a shot out the window at the bird. "I don't know why I had my bow and arrow in my room then," he adds with a laugh.

While the fabled Giants defense was an especially tight unit, most of those stars didn't pal around with the offensive players, but Livingston was a happy exception. "I went out with the guys from the offense because they were the guys who partied all the time," he says. "I was friends with everybody."

Livingston also fulfilled expectations by marrying a Playboy bunny, but defied them by lasting nearly forty years and counting with his wife, Linda. "She wouldn't have anything to do with me at first, but I persisted," Livingston says.

Livingston met Linda while he was with the Los Angeles Rams—he had been dumped by Allie Sherman after the 1961 season as part of Sherman's controversial overhauling of the Giants' vaunted defense. Livingston spent one season in Minnesota, where he was named defensive captain, an honor he enjoyed. But he got hurt and thought his playing days were done until former Giants roommate Harland Svare was named head coach of the Rams and traded for Livingston, after extracting a promise that Livingston wouldn't take advantage of his friendship. "He knew my habits and made me promise not to exploit him," Livingston says with a chuckle. "Harland extended my career by several years. It was a great opportunity for me in my 'golden years.'"

By 1965, Livingston was starting to "sour against the game"— looking back, he realized that he was unable to accept the fact that while he was still faster than many linebackers, he had lost a step or two. "It's too bad we can't play forever," he says, but he knew the time had come to leave the game.

After retiring, Livingston, who back in his college days had harbored thoughts of becoming a coach, instead left football for life as a commercial stunt man. "I had registered with a modeling agency on Hollywood Boulevard and they called me for a commercial for Schlitz Beer," he says. Livingston worked on about eighteen commercials over the next ten years, "making more money from doing one commercial than I would from playing football." (His daughter Paige is now a movie actress.)

During the mid-1970s, Livingston left acting behind to go to work for his brother, then a building contractor; he worked as a carpenter and then helped his brother run a couple of jobs. After a few years, Livingston and his family moved to Hawaii for about eight years, where he again worked as a carpenter.

The family returned in the 1980s and until his injury Livingston had been running his building maintenance business. The day he hurt himself, Livingston simply thought he had "tweaked" something, but his back started feeling progressively worse and soon his legs would go numb at certain times of day. That's when he went to the doctors, who told him he needed back surgery. During the three-and-a-half-hour operation surgeons had to extract several discs and insert cadaver bones and fuse them together.

These days, Livingston can't lift more than fifty or sixty pounds and returning to extremely physical work seems unlikely, a frustrating proposition for a man "who has always been active."

Since the surgery Livingston has been helping his wife manage a twenty-two-unit apartment complex and taking retraining classes for computers, which he finds challenging "because my memory is slipping a bit."

Not working has been taking its toll in part because Livingston acknowledges he "didn't plan well for my retirement" and in part because "I feel like I'm wasting away." Still, while he has been feeling "antsy as hell," Livingston is confident that things will improve. "I'll find something," he says. "There's lots of stuff I can do."

Dick Nolan has lived a full football life, from the game's highest highs to its lowest lows. He was part of the University of Maryland's greatest seasons, a defensive back on the Giants' 1956 championship team, and the first head coach to bring credibility to the San Francisco 49ers, but he was also the head coach of the New Orleans Saints when a front-office fiasco took a respectable team and turned it into a laughingstock. He has even seen his son Mike experience some of the same highs and lows in coaching.

But through it all, Nolan loved the game and tried to maintain an even keel. "No matter what happens, you have to do your job and just go with it," he says.

Back in high school and college, Dick Nolan played both offense and defense, as almost everyone did back in the 1940s and '50s. But while many of those two-way players hankered after the glory of life on offense, Nolan was perfectly happy playing defense. "I enjoyed hitting people," he says.

He liked not just the impact but the intimidation: Nolan's former partner in the Giants secondary, Tom Landry, used to tell of a game against the Los Angeles Rams when Deacon Dan Towler ran head-on into the goalpost and briefly blacked out. When he came to, Nolan was standing over him telling him, "Deacon, if you come my way again, I really am going to hit you. That was just a sample."

Nolan was born in Pittsburgh but moved to Chicago and Cleveland before his father, a Union Carbide executive, settled the family in White Plains. There, Nolan was all-county in football during high school, but he was also a standout as a catcher in baseball, which was his first love. In fact, Nolan was ready to jump at a minor league contract after his senior year when his father said, "Uh-uh, buddy. You're going to college."

It turned out to be a wise choice—at Maryland, Nolan not only developed as a football star, he also met his wife, Ann, to whom he has been married for over fifty years.

Nolan played a little quarterback as a freshman but ultimately made a name for himself as a halfback and defensive back. Nolan, who also ran the 100 and 220 in track for his fraternity to keep in shape, was part of two memorable seasons. In 1951, the team, led by Dick and Ed Modzelewski and future NFL Hall of Famer Stan Jones, went undefeated and even upset top-ranked Tennessee 28–13 in the Sugar Bowl. There was some unhappiness afterward because the bowl games did not count toward the national championship back then and Tennessee retained its crown. But Maryland had the favor returned in 1953 when Nolan and other future NFL players like Ralph Felton, Ron Waller, and Chet Hanulak led the Terps to their first national championship, even though their undefeated season ended in an upset 7–0 loss to Oklahoma in the Orange Bowl. "We did everything but put the ball across the goal line," Nolan recalls of a game in which several drives fell just short.

Nolan had started out studying engineering but switched to business administration after six months because engineering "took too much time. I couldn't do it." He did not count on an NFL career, and in fact when a friend came up to him one day at the dining hall and said, "Congratulations, you've been drafted," Nolan originally thought he was heading off into the Army.

Nolan was drafted by the Giants and spent two weeks on the offense before being sent to right cornerback, where he found himself in the secondary with Tom Landry. "He was a good guy and a good player," Nolan says. "He was not a speed merchant but he was smart." Nolan would learn from Landry and would eventually have his post-football career shaped by his fellow cornerback.

Nolan got off to a great start with what would prove a career-high six interceptions his rookie year. In the off-season at one point he got a job for a steel foundry in Baltimore. He started out as a "looper" in the foundry and worked his way up to sales, which was a relief because before that he'd come home every night with his face "as black as coal." The job paid well but the bosses wanted him to make it permanent.

In the end, Nolan couldn't do it. "When football season came around I said, 'Mr. Turner, I know I told you I'd stay, but I've just gotta go back,' and he said, 'Son, I wish I could go with you.'"

Nolan was a key component of the fabled defense on the 1956 championship team, but after the 1957 season he was traded to

Chicago for several players, including Pat Summerall. "It hurt leaving the Giants, but I went along with it," Nolan says. "It wasn't hard to adjust."

In 1958 he picked off five passes while with the Bears, and the next season the Giants reacquired him and again he swiped five balls in midair. "Pat used to joke that the Giants didn't like what they got in the trade for me so they went out and got me back again," Nolan says. "I was just glad they brought me back."

Life with the Giants was glorious in those days when it seemed like every starter was a star. Nolan met a representative from RJ Reynolds at a function, and, soon after, he got a call from the guy asking what brand of cigarettes he smoked. "I named every cigarette there was except Camel," Nolan says. "The guy asked if I'd smoke Camel and I said sure." Soon he was featured on a billboard on Broadway and was endorsing both Camel and Schick, doing cheek-to-cheek razor tests on the Jackie Gleason show.

By the end of the 1961 season, Nolan knew his career was winding down. Tom Landry knew it too. "He said to me, 'You're getting to be an old man, you should be coaching,'" Nolan recalls. Nolan wanted to play a little more, perhaps serve as a player-coach the way Landry had done for the Giants. Landry said sure, come to the new American Football League team in Dallas and do that. "But when I got off the plane to meet with him he said he just wanted me to coach."

Nolan accepted the idea and let his body go, putting on twenty-five pounds in the rest of the off-season. Then, on the day before the first game of the 1962 season, Landry, noting weaknesses and injuries in the secondary, said, "Would you like to play again?"

Nolan was shocked, saying, "But you talked me out of it. When do you want me to start?"

"Tomorrow," Landry replied.

"The next day it was 103 degrees in the Cotton Bowl and I felt like I lost all twenty-five pounds in the first quarter," Nolan says.

He served as a player-coach the rest of the season, then continued working for Landry, implementing different types of defenses. "We used the 4-3 defense but we took movements and put them together. We called it the flexible 4-3 and it got shortened to the flex defense."

Then, in 1968, the San Francisco 49ers came calling, looking for a head coach. The 49ers had been a second-rate franchise, reaching the playoffs only once before, in the 1950s. Nolan took over and brought his tough-minded defensive style along with a willingness to let quarterback John Brodie pursue a wide-open offense. By his third year, Nolan had helped create a newly competitive franchise—the team went 10-3-1 in 1970, going all the way to the conference championship. Nolan, who says he had felt confident of his abilities from his first day as head coach, was named coach of the year, but remembers feeling frustrated that the team didn't reach the Super Bowl. He lost to Tom Landry's Cowboys when his team couldn't control an on-side kick. Still, Nolan brought San Francisco back to the conference championship the following season and to the playoffs again in 1972 before stumbling through three lackluster years.

Then, three years after being fired by San Francisco, Nolan was called upon to bring order and respectability to another permanently frazzled franchise, the New Orleans Saints. Nolan was given a five-year deal for a reported $100,000 a year, a large sum at the time. For a while, it worked, as Nolan again mixed his emphasis on defense with Archie Manning's big-gun offense. Although there was some criticism that Nolan was too enamored with players who could master his complex flex defense regardless of whether they were the best players available, the Saints went 7-9 and then 8-8—the best record in their history—finishing second and almost making the playoffs in 1979. And then the trouble began. Saints owner, oil magnate, and known meddler John Mecom hired Steve Rosenbloom as general manager. The thirty-six-year-old Rosenbloom's sole qualification seemed to be that he was the son of the Los Angeles Rams' late owner Carroll Rosenbloom—he had been pushed out there in a power struggle with his stepmother.

"He didn't know too much about football, his dad was taking care of him," says Nolan, who soon found himself on the losing end of a power struggle with the front office. "He didn't know why he was doing the things he was doing. We slipped and slid after that."

Meanwhile, there were reports of drug problems, racial tensions, and, as the losses began mounting, of players giving up, and the fans were growing restless. After the team lost its seventh straight game, local fan Robert Le Compte designed a bag with eye slots and the word "Aints" on it, promising to wear the bag until the Saints won a game. Soon there were hundreds of people wearing bags at a nationally televised game. Nolan, who unfortunately became the public target for the fans' displeasure, would not be around to see that first win, as he was fired on November 24 after twelve straight losses—a day the team got beat 27–7 and had one play with ten guys on the field and another with twelve. Still, he never let up. "You have to do the best you could. I just ignored the fans—you can't let them think they're going to get to you."

Soon after, Rosenbloom was fired too.

Nolan ended up back in Texas as defensive coordinator for the Houston Oilers. At one point he was a leading candidate for the head coaching job at his alma mater in Maryland, but he says now he doesn't think he would have wanted to return to the college game. Eventually, he returned to Dallas, working for Landry until his death and then staying for two more years until he retired. These days, Nolan is content to work around his house just outside of Dallas and travel with Ann, going everywhere from Ireland to Australia. "We have a good time," he says.

But the Nolan defensive approach remained a constant in the NFL, even after his retirement. Nolan's son Mike has earned a strong reputation as defensive coordinator for his dad's old team, the Giants, under Dan Reeves, then for the Washington Redskins and now the Baltimore Ravens. "Mike used to sit in on my meetings as a kid," Nolan says. "He learned a heck of a lot, I guess—he knows his football."

It must run in the family.

Alex Webster didn't make the cut. Football was finished for this North Carolina State star tailback—he was going back home to Kearny, New Jersey, and his job at Otis Elevators.

Webster had been drafted by the Washington Redskins in 1953, but coach Curly Lambeau stuck him at safety. Still, it looked like Webster—who had planned on teaching one day and never dreamed of making it to the NFL—was going to make the team. "They cut the squad down to thirty-three and I had survived the last cut," he recalls. "I was looking for an apartment in Washington."

But the finger of fate was feeling fickle that week. On the Thursday before the season began, the Redskins managed to land veteran defensive back Don Doll from Detroit, and suddenly Webster was gone. "They gave me $10 to catch a train to Newark, but then I still had to take a bus home," he recalls. "It was heartbreaking."

It was actually a good move for Washington as Doll picked off ten passes that year, but in the end it would be even better news for the New York Giants, of course. But Webster had no way of knowing stardom awaited. As far as he was concerned, football was in the past. "That was it," he says. "Where was I going to go?"

Then he ran into an old friend from high school who was then working as an assistant sports editor for the *Newark Star-Ledger*. "He said 'What are you doing here?' And when I told him, he said, 'You've got to play somewhere,'" Webster recalls. The editor sent an overnight telegram to Montreal in the Canadian Football League. Webster got a phone call the next morning, and, after borrowing money from his family, he was up in Montreal that afternoon—the last day teams were allowed to sign "American imports."

The season was nearly half over, but Webster played fairly well. The next season, however, he soared, becoming the Alouettes' leading rusher and receiver, sparking the team to a league-leading 348 points scored on the way to the Grey Cup game. But Webster and his wife Louise had had their first child while he was in Montreal, and he was a bit homesick and also sick of being under-paid—he was offered $7,500, less than his two Canadian backfield mates, who also had full-time local jobs. (The teams practiced at night so players could work year-round at regular jobs.)

Webster threatened to go back to the NFL, to which, he says, the general manager sneered, "You didn't make it the first time, you're not going to make it the second time." But several American teams had noticed Webster's performance, including the Lions, the Red-skins, and the Giants, whose scout Al Derogatis had sent words of praise to the Maras. Webster knew he didn't want to return to Washington, so he went in to meet with Wellington Mara and ended up signing a deal.

The league was indeed different—and not just because Canada had more quirky rules. "The players in Canada were not as big, so that was a change for me," he says.

But the Giants' offensive coach was Vince Lombardi, and he per-sonally transformed Webster's career. "He's the one who pushed me into becoming a fairly good player," Webster recalls. "I was lazy but he stayed on my butt the whole time."

Webster, who lived at home at first, quickly established himself as a force in the league. As a rookie, he scored six touchdowns while averaging 5.0 yards per carry in 128 attempts and 12.2 yards in his twenty-two catches. He went on to score ten touchdowns during the championship season of 1956. Webster would go on to make all-pro three times, but he struggled with leg injuries from 1958 through 1960, a year in which he made only twenty-two car-ries. But he bounced back to prove himself once again when new coach Allie Sherman moved him to fullback in 1961. "That was a blessing for me, but I also got myself in the best shape of my ca-reer," he says. Webster gained a career-high 928 yards, averaging 4.7 yards per carry, while also catching twenty-six passes for an-other 313 yards. He again surpassed 1,200 total yards the following year before slowing down in his final two seasons—the last one being that infamous and disastrous 1964 season that began the "Goodbye, Allie" chants that would echo around the stadium for years.

"That was a tough year—we took a hell of a beating," Webster says. "I think a lot of us hung on too long. We could have gone out on top a year or so earlier. You always think you have one more year left in you."

When he had first arrived at the Giants, Webster had found off-season and even in-season work with Ballantine Brewery, doing everything from driving and unloading trucks to sales. "I worked my butt off," he says.

But after he retired, Webster worked for a printing company while also giving a try as the color analyst for the Giants games on WNEW on the radio. "That was hard. I couldn't pick it up at all," Webster says, adding that while the then low pay left little incentive to stick around, the job eventually became quite lucrative. That job and the money, of course, went to his teammate and friend Dick Lynch, but Webster says he was the right man for it. "He's a good guy and, boy, he can talk."

Webster, who had moved to East Brunswick and would by the end of the 1960s move to Sea Girt on the Jersey shore (former summer spot for Tim Mara and future summer spot for Bill Parcells), then spent a year doing a postgame show on television before Allie Sherman invited him back to the sidelines as the backfield coach. "I really enjoyed those two years as an assistant," Webster says.

Then everything changed in 1970. One day coming back from an exhibition game, Webster and Sherman had what he calls "a good discussion" about the direction of the team. While he says it was not a big argument, he adds, "I started shooting my mouth off." So, the next day, when he was called in to the Giants' offices for a meeting, Webster expected he was going to be axed.

"I went in with my golf outfit on, thinking I'd get fired and then go play golf," he says. But unlike his first experience in the NFL with Washington, this time he wasn't cut—instead, he learned that Sherman was being let go and that Webster was the new Giants head coach. "I spent most of the day sitting and talking with Wellington."

But while he was honored to be hired, he thinks that in retrospect it was the wrong choice, both for him and for the Giants. "The toughest years I ever had were as head coach," he says. "I had no experience and didn't know anything."

While he said he was comfortable running an offense and calling plays, he says he didn't know how to deal with the business side of running a team and had a hard time running a disciplined team.

"I treated them like I would have wanted to be treated as a person," he says—despite the fact that he had credited Lombardi's hectoring with making him a success. "I wasn't strict. That's the trouble. I gave them a free hand and you can't do that."

The players responded well the first year, when Ron Johnson's Webster-like running performance led the team to a 9-5 record. "I had a good time that year," Webster says. But with the front office failing to provide fresh talent and Webster losing control of the players, the team began to struggle, falling to 4-10, then bouncing back to 8-6, and then, finally, after a 6-0 exhibition season in 1973, the team—stuck playing several home games up in Connecticut—collapsed with a 2-11-1 record. "It took a lot out of me," he says, adding that the media's constant "digging"—the constant nagging questions that seemed to be trying to get him to publicly criticize his players—also wore on him.

"Afterwards I felt relieved. I felt like I came back to life again," he says, adding that throughout the experience he felt that the Mara family treated him well and fairly. With coaching behind him, Webster went to work for former teammate Ralph Guglielmi, who had been a backup to Y. A. Tittle at quarterback in 1962 and 1963, and who hired Webster to help sell business supplies and computer forms to businesses. "I was learning on the job, but the big thing was I knew so many people," he says.

Webster really found his niche in his next job, working in public relations for Standard Brands, which was later bought out by Nabisco and then RJ Reynolds. "I had a great run there for twelve years," he says. "It was a lot of work—and a lot of travel, that was the tough part—but I played a lot of golf too."

He also endured a lot of surgery—four trips to different surgeons for a slipped disc injury before finding a doctor in Cleveland who resolved the problem in the late 1980s—and although he has some arthritic pain, he can still play golf and get around okay.

In the early 1990s, under Nabisco, Webster was asked to transfer to a new office in Jupiter, Florida. "We already had a condo in North Palm Beach and my wife said yes before I could even say anything," Webster says.

However, while he was still coaching, Webster had also found another role, as a restaurateur, opening up a bar and restaurant four blocks from his home in Sea Girt. The name, The Stadium, came about inadvertently. Webster had asked Mara if during the off-season the coaches could work out of offices in Yankee Stadium instead of going to the team headquarters at 10 Columbus Circle, where they had to pay for parking and dress for the business world in a shirt and tie. Mara called Yankees executive Lee MacPhail, who invited him to look for space underneath the stadium. His search revealed storage areas packed with old pictures, trophies, and other memorabilia, some of which hadn't been opened in decades. So when Webster was opening the restaurant he asked MacPhail if he could buy one or two items; MacPhail said to just take whatever he wanted. "That worked out pretty nicely," Webster says, explaining that they decorated the entire restaurant in Yankees and Giants memorabilia.

By the time Webster was moving to Florida, his business partner in the restaurant was ready to retire, but after selling the popular New Jersey restaurant, he decided he wanted to give it another go in Florida. Webster was game too, but it didn't work, lasting only two years. The Tequester-based place, Alex Webster's, offered linen napkins and tablecloths and, Webster says, did fine in winter when New Yorkers abounded but proved too fancy and expensive for locals to support the rest of the year. "Still, I got to meet a lot of people down here right after moving," he says.

After being laid off in a round of corporate maneuverings at RJ Reynolds, Webster retired. "Try to get a job at that age," he says. "It's just impossible."

So Webster sold his large house and moved to a smaller place in Hope Sound where the taxes are cheaper and the walls are built twelve inches thick with cement to withstand any hurricanes.

For a guy who had, once upon a time, given up on pro football, it has all turned out just fine.

On the field, as a defensive back, Erich Barnes was known for tackling opponents with a passion, a ferocity that few others could match. But off the field, Barnes is a low-key guy, a pragmatist with a hearty laugh and great equanimity, who doesn't worry about events beyond his control.

Barnes grew up in Indiana in a large, happy family. He played sports, but it wasn't a central focus in his life, and to the extent that sports mattered, basketball mattered most, as you would imagine out in Hoosier-land. In fact, Barnes, who did football, basketball, and track in high school, says he got into Purdue on a hoops scholarship, for his play at guard and shooting forward. "I never saw a shot I didn't like," he says.

But when Barnes entered Purdue in the 1950s, he didn't have any sort of athletic career in mind. "At that time going to the pros wasn't as big an issue—there just weren't that many African-Americans playing professional sports," he says, pointing out that most NFL teams had no more than three or four black players. "There was nothing there to look forward to. I wanted to be a teacher and maybe a coach."

Yet Barnes's life soon shifted tracks. For starters, he found greater success on the gridiron than on the basketball court. And, he soon realized, "the more I played the less and less I wanted to coach—it wasn't as easy as it looks." (He feels that way even more strongly today, with the shift in attitudes among young players creating a roster with "fifty players who all think they're stars.")

He was also realizing that he had what it took to play in the NFL. "By my sophomore year I felt I had mastered the defensive back position and knew I could play it in the pros," he says. While he also played halfback in college, Barnes knew he preferred life in the defensive secondary. "It's a good, strategic position that required a lot of skills, but it's also relatively safe and injury free," he says. "When you're a running back, too many people get a shot at you."

Barnes was drafted by the Chicago Bears before the 1958 season, and he flourished quickly upon his arrival, finishing second on the team with four pick-offs in his rookie year and tying for the team lead with five the following year. Suddenly Barnes found himself not only an established NFL player but also a Pro Bowler . . . and, soon after, he found himself shipped out of town. The Bears had a strong defense but needed someone to take the helm offensively, and after the 1960 season they constructed a three-team deal with Los Angeles and New York in which Barnes, who'd had no interceptions that year, ended up with the Giants and Chicago pocketed quarterback Billy Wade. (In 1963, Wade helped lead the Bears to the NFL championship over the Giants in the title game.)

The young star was neither shocked nor distressed. He simply packed his bags and moved on. "I knew how the system worked and I'd had good mentors so I understood this was a business first," he says, adding that millions of Americans get job transfers that require them to move.

And, he adds, "players at the top of their game are always up for a trade—the Bears needed a quarterback more." The Giants, on the other hand, needed a defensive back to complement Dick Lynch. "I came in at the right time," he says of helping spark the team to three more championship games in the early 1960s. "The guys were really nice—we all became buddies quickly."

Barnes stepped up his play with his new club, earning Pro Bowl status in each of his four years in New York and coming up with numerous big plays at big moments along the way. In 1961, he nabbed seven opponents' passes. In a game against 3-1 Dallas that the 3-1 Giants needed to win to remain in a tie in the Eastern Division, Barnes came up with two interceptions, most memorably one on a play in the third quarter with the team holding a 17–10 lead but with the Cowboys on the verge of scoring.

Barnes grabbed an Eddie LeBaron pass headed for Jim Doran in the right corner of the end zone and raced the length of the field along the sideline for a 102-yard interception touchdown return, tying the then NFL record. (Some folks said it was really 103 yards, which is actually now the new record, although arguably once you're in your own end zone it's pretty much all the same.)

"Cliff Livingston gave me a look and said, let's go," Barnes recalls. "When you're in the end zone all you want to do is get out 20 yards."

The moment that sticks out the most came once he was in the

clear, when "Don Meredith tried to trip me from the sidelines," Barnes recalls with a chuckle, adding that "Dallas on a 110-degree day was not the best place to have a run like that, though."

The following year, during the 16–7 loss in the NFL championship game against Green Bay, Barnes produced the only Giants score, with the team trailing 10–0, when he blocked a Packer punt in the end zone and Jim Collier recovered for a touchdown.

But for Barnes it was never about the highlights. "I enjoyed playing from week to week. I always did the best I could and I always felt comfortable out there," he says.

Beyond his notable plays—Barnes had eighteen interceptions in four years with the Giants—throughout his career he had a reputation as one of the league's most intimidating defensive backs, one of the hardest hitters around. Clean and legal but ultra-tough. He was called "King of the Clothesline" by some, the sort of guy who kept opposing receivers fearful about running routes across the middle.

Barnes says it was just that at 6'3" and 200 pounds he was much larger than most other guys playing his position. "It wasn't so much that I hit harder than anybody else at cornerback, it's just that I was bigger so I did more damage," he says, adding that he didn't injure anyone, always hitting high in part for safety and in part because he felt it gave him a better chance to jar a pass loose than did hitting someone at the knees. "That's where you should hit guys," he says.

But after his four straight Pro Bowl trips, Barnes was traded yet again in yet another three-team deal for—you guessed it—another quarterback. In 1965 the thirty-year-old star was sent off to Cleveland so the Giants, who had stumbled badly in 1964, could acquire Earl Morrall from Detroit. Again, Barnes had no complaints.

"When they called to tell me, I said, 'That's good,' and I packed my clothes and left," he says.

For starters, he knew the 2-12 Giants were a team in rapid decline; additionally, he had grown up a Cleveland Browns fan, so there was a certain thrill in going back to the Midwest; and, finally, Barnes, who would go on to play another seven years, knew that most football players didn't even have careers that lasted half of his fourteen-year career, much less manage to stay in one place. "I never had any animosity toward the Giants," he says. "They were all good people, especially the Maras."

Barnes didn't let up in Cleveland, with four interceptions and a return average of 32 yards in 1966, a return to the Pro Bowl in 1968, and five more interceptions in his thirteenth year in 1970 among other highlights. In 1971 he played only three games, then retired with forty-five career interceptions returned for a total of 853 yards and seven touchdowns.

Back in Chicago early in his career, Barnes had taught during the off-season, fulfilling his original career plan, but in Cleveland he had opened a small sports consulting business about four years before his career ended, and after he retired he just kept going with that, advising companies on sports marketing and "how to associate their businesses with sports and people in the sports world." Barnes always kept the company small—"it was a low-profile thing"—and about five years ago he moved back east to Yonkers to semi-retire and work exclusively for one company that had provided much of his business. Now he is largely retired, although besides fishing, golf, and tennis, Barnes keeps plenty busy doing volunteer work for various charities, particularly those that are offshoots of the NFL Players Association and NFL Alumni association.

Barnes says he still gets about two hundred letters a year from Purdue, Chicago, New York, and Cleveland fans, many of whom call to say they think he should be enshrined in the Pro Football Hall of Fame. Barnes knows that despite his credentials, it isn't likely—"you've got to promote yourself, you've got to be a politician, and I'm not going to do all that," he says.

There are overlooked and quiet players who do get in, like the recently elected Carl Eller, but that defensive star had the backing of an aggressive promotional campaign pushed by the Minnesota Vikings ownership. Eller, of course, played his whole career for one team, while Barnes went from one team to another. "No one [from those teams] is going to devote that kind of time and energy to a guy like me. They've got their own guys to worry about," he says, adding matter-of-factly, "You can't blame anybody for the situation." Still, he adds with yet another laugh, "If it were up to me, I'd vote for myself."

The Downward Spiral

Allie Sherman 🏈

He was just some little scrawny lefty quarterback from Brownsville, too small to try out for his high school football team, never more than a backup in the pros. Yet Allie Sherman ended up front and center for some of the highest highs and lowest lows in Giants history. As the backfield coach and then head coach, he helped lead the Giants to one title game after another, but he didn't adapt well as the team aged and made the crucial mistake of trading the still popular and effective Sam Huff, leading to the fans' trying to boo him out of town.

Sherman has also had several unusual gigs since his days with the Giants, and he'll tell it all to you in the greatest of detail. As a raconteur, he's like a great running back—give him the smallest opening and he'll blast through, carrying you on his back for forty, fifty, sixty yards worth of yarns.

Sherman was born in 1923 in Brownsville and moved at age six to where the IRT ends in New Lots, where he played endless hours of sandlot football at a place called Tiger Field before his family moved up in the world to Eastern Parkway in Crown Heights—then he would continue to trek out to Tiger Field to play in the mornings before coming home in the afternoon to play at the Parade Grounds, eventually starring for a top-notch local team called the Dukes. (He remained in his family's apartment until he started playing in the NFL for Philadelphia.) He recalls that the neighborhood was dominated by apartments except for an area by President Street where there were private homes with "lawns the size of postage stamps" that nonetheless seemed to Sherman like "it was out in the country."

"I would walk out of my way just to see those homes," he recalls, adding that as an adult he eventually fulfilled his childhood dream by moving to the Westchester suburbs.

Sherman skipped grades, graduating from Boys High School at sixteen, so it was not surprising that the 150-pound underage student was told by coach Wally Muller that he was too small to even try out. Muller instead sent him to play handball, and he was the number two singles player on the school's city-championship-winning team in 1938.

Still, he kept sharp playing on the sandlots, and as a walk-on at Brooklyn College he started as a freshman. There he played tailback in the single wing but then moved to quarterback as an early pioneer in the T formation after the Chicago Bears won the NFL championship with this surprising new innovation. (Sherman learned the T while working in the Catskills over the summer—his coach would send him a new chapter each week from a book on the new formation.)

As a senior, Sherman had his biggest moment at the right time—in his last game, an exhibition against City College to raise money for City College, during which he threw for two touchdowns and ran for two more while leading the team to victory after a 20–0 halftime deficit. "Twelve days later I got a questionnaire from the Eagles, who were looking for T-formation quarterback," he says.

Still, times were tough. This was 1943, during World War II, and Philadelphia and Pittsburgh had to merge their teams into the "Steeglers" just to have a full roster. "I was earning $125 a game," Sherman says, "and was probably the first pro athlete to write home saying, "Please send money," just so I could afford to keep playing."

For five years, Sherman was a backup quarterback and played his fair share of defense, paying attention to both sides of the game since by then he knew that he wanted to be a coach. Eagles coach Greasy Neale was "like a surrogate father. I learned so much from him."

When the Eagles created a farm team, the Patterson (New Jersey) Panthers, Neale sent Sherman to coach—even though the young athlete balked at giving up his playing career and leaving the NFL. Neale convinced him that it would provide credibility, and Sherman soothed his ego and earned extra cash by both playing quarterback and coaching. Although he won there, Neale didn't find room for him, so Sherman came back home in 1949 when New York's Steve Owen hired him as backfield coach to teach the T formation to his other coaches and to a new quarterback, Charley Conerly. Although Conerly was a "taciturn Southerner," he and the garrulous Brooklynite clicked, and the Giants did too.

But five years later, when Sherman was at the hospital where his first child had just been born, he got a call from the Maras saying that Owen was retiring and that fellow assistant Jim Lee Howell, not Sherman, was getting the head job. So Sherman again left home for the one place he could find head coaching experience, the Canadian Football League's Winnipeg Blue Bombers. But after his second child was born a few years later, Sherman wanted to come home, and his close friend Marty Glickman—who had also introduced Sherman to his wife, Joan—helped arrange in 1959 for him to succeed Vince Lombardi as head offensive coach. Two years later, Sherman finally became head coach, after what seemed like forever although he was still only thirty-eight. He was named NFL Coach of the Year for each of his first two years and won three consecutive Eastern Conference titles. But several players say Sherman was intimidated by all those larger-than-life Giants heroes and let his insecurities force him into bad decisions, poorly handled. After trading Huff, the Giants collapsed, and during the dismal 1-12 1966 season, fans continually harassed him with chants of "Goodbye, Allie."

Sherman partially redeemed himself with three successive second-place finishes, but in 1969 he was finally fired. He spent five years as an investment advisor at the Wall Street firm Sanford Bernstein, but he knew he didn't want his career to be as some "glad-handing ex-jock." Instead, he poured increasing amounts of energy into television and marketing—he had his own show on WPIX, working with Glickman as his producer, while he was coaching, and he knew that could succeed there. "I had a pretty good feel for this kind of thing," he says.

He was friends with Steve Ross, who was running what was then Warner Communications (later Warner Amex and then Time Warner), and went to work as a consultant, helping get the fledgling cable business started. He worked with everyone from cable operators to program providers to advertisers to create alliances for the company, advised on sports programming—one idea that was clearly ahead of its time: he tried launching all-sports regional cable networks in Houston and two other markets—and helped launch the company's first pay-per-view efforts, beginning with its 1980 debut, a legendary welterweight championship bout between Sugar Ray Leonard and Roberto Duran.

Sherman's role even involved helping market the company's soccer team, the New York Cosmos. Among his bigger successes in attempting to build excitement and support among immigrants was providing bus rides from the city out to the Meadowlands, since many of those fans did not have cars. "I did everything but coach," he says, "since the ball has a different shape."

In the 1980s, Sherman returned to the public eye, becoming one of the earliest personalities on the tiny start-up known as ESPN, serving with Steve Sabol as a football analyst on the network's *Monday Night Match-up,* a program that lasted seven years. Then in the 1990s, he found himself in a more unusual job when Mayor Rudolph Giuliani named him as head of Off-Track Betting Corp. Although he failed to transform OTB and make it profitable and privatized, he says he remains on as an advisor in addition to consulting with several NFL teams.

More than three decades and three careers later, Sherman says the wounds have faded on the bad times as coach of the Giants, but the glow of the triumph still lingers. "Today, people remember the good years more than the bad years."

Yes, of course, linebacker Jerry Hillebrand had a rewarding career, especially that first year, when he won a starting job, intercepted five passes, and helped spark the Giants to the NFL championship game. He's not the complaining type, not one to dwell too much on the past, but now that you mention it, there are just two things he can't help regretting: he really wanted to play offense and he never should have retired when he did.

To be honest, Hillebrand didn't even settle on the tight end idea until after his sophomore year at college. That's not to say that sports, and football, weren't always central in his life. Growing up in Davenport, Iowa, the son of a beer salesman and a secretary, Hillebrand would tag along with older brothers Dick and Ken, playing football and baseball with the big kids. But his favorite sport was basketball—he was a center and forward, earning all-state honors and averaging twenty-two points per game in high school. It was his hoops skills as much as his play at center, linebacker, and defensive line that paved the way for him at the University of Colorado. "I went there to play both basketball and football," he says. "But when my grades started to suffer freshman year I had to choose one sport."

Football had two advantages: he was already bulking up past the 200-pound mark, "which made it a little tough getting up and down the basketball court," and the football coaching staff—known for one of the first spread-out passing games in the Big Eight—sweetened the deal: "They said they'd move me to end instead of center on offense so I'd get to touch the ball a little bit."

By the beginning of his junior year, Hillebrand had filled out further, the additional 30 pounds taking him up near 240, in an era when big, strong tight ends like Mike Ditka were becoming commonplace. Hillebrand looked around at the players he'd competed with who had been drafted and "I thought to myself, 'Maybe I've got a chance to be a tight end in the NFL.'"

But after his senior year when the Giants made him their top draft choice, they told him they'd selected him simply "as a player" and would define his role later on. "I preferred tight end but I would have played wherever they needed me, even offensive tackle, just to make it," he says. "It just so happened that a couple of our linebackers got hurt and I won the starting job at left linebacker."

At first, Hillebrand, one of the few rookies to make that veteran, long-standing unit, had been a bit overwhelmed. "It was very intimidating in training camp being with all these guys I'd been watching on television," he says. "I felt like a real youngster."

But the Giants defense preferred welcoming the newcomer to hazing him. "There was no harassment—they made me feel very comfortable," he says, adding that not only did he learn a great deal from his teammates, but they made the transition to the pro game much easier: "Having Jim Katcavage in front of you and Erich Barnes behind you and Sam Huff next to you provides pretty good protection."

To this day, however, Hillebrand wonders what might have been: "The only thing I wish is that I could have gotten to play tight end," he says. But having played the position in college definitely helped him handle opposing tight ends as a linebacker. "Having played the position, I knew how they released from their stance, the pass patterns they ran, and what they were thinking," he says. (But while being a two-way player in school provided a better understanding of the game, he adds, "it sure was tiring.")

Hillebrand moved to Queens, rooming with a college teammate who had been working in advertising and "who knew all the places to go and what to do." After he married, Hillebrand then followed Dick Lynch out to Douglaston.

But while it had been a thrill to join such a great defensive unit, it was a short-lived thrill. After the team lost the NFL championship when Y. A. Tittle got injured, coach Allie Sherman cleaned house, packing off legends Sam Huff and Dick Modzelewski, among others. Hillebrand was moved into Huff's old spot at middle linebacker. "I hated to see him go, but it was an honor for me to replace him," Hillebrand recalls. "The media put a little pressure on, but I didn't worry about trying to fill his shoes—I knew it would never be 'Violent World of Jerry Hillebrand,' put it that way."

Most frustrating, especially for a player like Hillebrand, who had

played for winners—his high school team once won thirty-three straight games—was the team's rapid decline. And Hillebrand eventually clashed with Sherman too. "We just didn't see eye to eye," he recalls. After 1966, "he said to me finally, 'I don't know what I'm going to do with you,' and I said, 'So trade me.'"

Hillebrand went to talk to Wellington Mara, who gently asked where he'd like to be traded. Hillebrand said somewhere in the Midwest, closer to home, and soon found himself in St. Louis. "I hated to leave New York but I appreciated that the Maras would do anything they could for you."

Hillebrand injured his knee in St. Louis and departed after one season for Pittsburgh in 1968, where former Giant Bill Austin was coaching. But then Chuck Knoll took over in 1969 and began a youth movement—rebuilding the team with young players named Joe Greene, L. C. Greenwood, Terry Bradshaw, Mel Blount, and then for the 1971 season, a linebacker by the name of Jack Ham— and Hillebrand was released.

It was a pivotal moment for Hillebrand. He had offers from San Diego and San Francisco to come try out, and he wanted to go, but his wife wanted him to stay put in Davenport instead, focusing on the work he had been doing in the off-season in his brother Dick's construction company. "She said, 'You've got a good job now, so why don't you hang them up,'" he recalls. "I didn't want to but she pulled more weight than I did, so I hung 'em up. I've regretted it ever since."

Although he doesn't see friends from his football days too often, living near Route 80 in Davenport does bring its share of visitors. "I get people going west or east all the time—I get calls from people I haven't heard from in years. Just a few months ago I got together with Al Gursky, who played with the Giants in 1963. I haven't seen him since then."

Hillebrand did do well in the construction business, working as a salesman, negotiating deals for his brother's company. "I had some old friends from New York who were putting up some res-taurants and since I had the connection we got the first shot at it," he says. And, when things were slow on the sales front, he'd work as a supervisor, running the actual construction jobs.

"It was a lot of fun, but there were a few jobs where things went wrong—it was like missing Jimmy Brown going down the sideline at Yankee Stadium. It was a tough job in football and it was a tough job in construction," he says. "But construction was not always the fairest game—the field was not always level for everyone."

Hillebrand, whose son and daughter also still live in Davenport, stuck with construction on and off—with a brief diversion into the recreation business, when he ran a roller-skating facility—until he retired, selling off the land on the fifty-unit senior housing project he had developed. "Now I just live in the condo and play a little golf," he says.

Everybody slows down a bit as they get older. That's perfectly normal, a natural part of aging. But for Homer Jones, the decline has been so steep as to seem almost cruel and unfair—the fleetest Giant ever, a man who could race 89 yards for a touchdown, now has trouble walking even 20 yards assisted by a cane. But Jones, who retains a dry humor even when discussing his ailments, is optimistic that he may once more be picking up speed.

Jones still lives in the tiny town of Pittsburg, Texas, where he grew up. He was an only child, the son of a steel mill worker and a schoolteacher. In junior high and high school, Jones played basketball and ran track—he never even took up football until his senior year. "I was in demand," he explains, adding that he finally joined the team not because of any grand plan but "because it was just another fun thing to do."

With his combination of speed and size, Jones soon found that football was more than mere fun and games—it earned him a scholarship to Texas Southern University in Houston, where he immediately "set my sights on making it to the pros." Jones, who had played fullback in high school, moved to wingback in college but says, "My position really didn't matter." In college he also ran a 9.3 in the 100-yard dash and was part of a relay team that won the conference championship, capturing the attention of both the NFL and the fledgling American Football League.

After college, both the Giants and the Houston Oilers of the AFL drafted Jones. Opting to stay close to home, Jones went with the Oilers, only to be rejected when he failed their physical because of bad knees—looking back, Jones says there were plenty of aches and pains during college and his days with the Giants that were likely early indicators of arthritis, but he did not know it back then. So Jones turned to the Giants, who, though they had taken him way down in the twentieth round, welcomed him and arranged for surgery, recuperation, and then workouts while on the team's taxi squad for the 1963 season.

Having lived in Houston for four years, Jones found adjusting to New York relatively easy—he lived first at the Grand Concourse Hotel and then "way up in the East Bronx." What he found "rather shocking" was how quickly the team's fortunes plummeted in 1964, his first year on the active roster. But Jones spent that year stuck behind Del Shofner anyway. It wasn't until 1965 that he would make his mark on the Giants—and leave a lasting impression on the game of football as a whole.

When he turned pro, Jones had promised himself that when he scored his first touchdown he'd hurl the ball into the stands in celebration. "I had watched Frank Gifford and the other guys do it and I said, 'One of these days I'm going to be able to do it.'"

But in 1964 Jones caught only four passes and didn't score. He spent more time proving himself on special teams, where he used his phenomenal speed to get downfield and throw two key blocks on Clarence Childs's historic 100-yard kickoff return. (He also made a name for himself by challenging Y. A. Tittle to throw balls far downfield and outracing them every time.)

Then, he says, "that off-season they changed the rule—Mr. Rozelle said you couldn't throw the ball into the stands." Rozelle backed the rule up with a $500 fine. Still, Jones wanted to figure out something for when the magic moment arrived.

Although Jones still wasn't a primary target in the offense, he brought that moment to life the next season. On October 17, 1965, against the Philadelphia Eagles, the Giants found themselves at their own 11-yard line on Jones's first play from scrimmage. He grabbed a pass from Earl Morrall, raced 89 yards untouched into the end zone, and, in his moment of triumph, hurled the ball to the ground. The spike was born.

Jones doesn't even recall whether the fans or foes reacted at all to his celebration. "The whole thing just happened from the line of scrimmage—boom, boom, boom—and all I heard was all of Yankee Stadium in an uproar."

The spike became Jones's signature play as he scored thirty-three more times over the next four years. Gradually, of course, others copied it and then expanded on it from dances by the likes of Billy "White Shoes" Johnson on down to Terrell Owens's pulling out a Sharpie to sign the ball.

Jones never topped his first spike for sheer exuberance, but he would go on to top his long catch the following year on September 11 against Pittsburgh with a Giants-record 98-yard touchdown catch. "We were backed up against the end zone," Jones says, but he told quarterback Earl Morrall that the defense was "ready to pluck" and Morrall should heave the ball as far as he could. "He threw it 55 yards in the air and I caught it on the dead run," Jones says.

That was the year Jones broke the 1,000-yard mark, and his career would soar still higher after the arrival of Fran Tarkenton at quarterback, as he achieved Pro Bowl status in 1967 and 1968—no Giants receiver since has managed to do it even once. In 1967, the blur in number 45 averaged an astonishing 24.7 yards per catch, set a club record with 1,209 yards caught that would last thirty years, and led the league with thirteen touchdowns scored; the following year he surpassed 1,000 yards again and averaged over 23 yards per catch. His numbers slipped a bit in 1969 but were still solid. Jones was slowing down, but he still had one more bit of magic left in him.

With the Cleveland Browns in 1970, Jones caught only ten passes, but he returned twenty-nine kicks, including one that added another footnote to his historical record—on September 21 he returned the second-half kickoff 94 yards for a touchdown, becoming the first person to run back a kick for a touchdown, on the new telecast called *Monday Night Football*.

When Jones retired, he had the NFL's highest average gain per reception for a career at 22.3 yards, a mark that still stands, and was third in total yards caught for the Giants, although he has since been surpassed by Joe Morrison and Armani Toomer. Jones, who had done some cattle farming back home during the off-seasons, returned to Pittsburg after his playing days ended, but he also traveled quite a bit working as a greeter for American Express. "My job was to meet the public. I'd go to parties, the Super Bowl, the Pro Bowl—I was getting paid to have fun," he says.

In 1973, one year after his father retired from the steel mill, Jones took a job there, settling down and helping to raise his six children. But the arthritis began taking more and more of a toll and, in 1992, Jones was forced quit his job and go on disability—at first the NFL rejected his NFL disability requests, although that was eventually settled, and between that and his pension he now has enough to live on. But things would only get tougher—in 1993, his father died and, two years later, Jones's home burned down, destroying virtually all his photos and other mementos from his college and Giants days.

"It was tough," he says. "They had real sentimental value and were things you think you'd never lose, things that would be with you your whole life."

The arthritis hurts everywhere—the shoulders, knees, and elbows, but the worst part of all has long been his hip. He thought about hip replacement surgery in the 1990s but backed out: "It was supposed to happen but I was a little leery of it," he says, explaining that he has a phobia of hospitals (and another of flying—he hasn't flown since the American Express days).

So Jones just kept toughing it out, watching NFL games on television, puttering in his garden, and shopping at flea markets and garage sales. "I have an addiction to junk," he says with a laugh.

"Space here is getting limited," he adds. "I just bought a storage building for some of the stuff. Maybe I should have my own garage sale."

But the arthritis has "grown a little worse every year," until the point that Jones, who gained a good deal of weight as his mobility declined, says, "there are times where I'm not even able to walk 20 yards with a cane anymore. It's a painful thing."

So 2005 should be the year that he finally braves the hospital for the hip replacement surgery. "I'd just like to able to walk," he says, adding that if he can move without a cane he might be able to go fishing again. Having enough mobility for fishing and flea markets, he concludes, "might be incentive enough to get me into the hospital this time."

C larence Childs didn't go to college to play football, he played football to go to college—the scholarship he earned thanks to his athletic skills enabled him to become the first person in his family to go to college. And while he went on to play pro football, when his playing days were over he went back to college . . . for thirty-five more years, eventually rising to become vice president for student affairs at Bethune-Cookman College.

Childs grew up in small-town Lakeland, Florida; his parents were common laborers, but he spent a great deal of time living with his grandparents. "Everybody took care of everybody back then," he says. The family never had a car until he made it to the NFL, so they walked or rode the lackluster Lakeland bus system, and they never got more than two or three presents for Christmas. "That's just the way it was—we never felt impoverished," he says, adding that that sort of upbringing helped build character. "You wouldn't get new stuff, so you learned to take care of what you had."

He adds that his grandmother also helped keep him out of trouble and focused on school—where he was always told that if his grades suffered, he would not be allowed to play sports. "My grandmother was a very religious woman," he says. "I had to be in church every time they opened the doors—I was on the usher board, in the choir. She believed that birds of a feather flocked together and didn't want me hanging out with the wrong kids."

Childs had an older and a younger brother, but neither was interested in sports. And he viewed himself more as a baseball player than as a football player—after all, even when he grew up and reached the Giants he only weighed in at around 180 pounds. But it was his football playing at running back, defensive back, and even quarterback that earned him a scholarship to Florida A&M. When he got there, the baseball coach asked him to come out for that team too, but Childs instead opted for track—it wasn't about preferring one sport over another, it was all about academics.

"The baseball team traveled too much—they'd play forty or fifty games and have trips out west, and I didn't want to get caught up in just being a baseball player," recalls the former major. "But the track team had meets only on weekends, so you didn't have to miss any classes. And a couple of us would even carry our books with us to the meets."

Childs was a two-time champion in the 220-yard dash, but he adds that the track team was filled with stars from an extremely talented Rattler football team—"we had ten guys on that team who could run the 100-yard dash in 9.8 or better." The team went undefeated twice in his four years there, with Childs twice winning the MVP award in the Orange Blossom Classic.

The team's coach used to send out three distinct units or "waves"—the Blood, the Sweat, and the Tears waves. "Most of those guys could have started at other schools, and each group was always trying to outdo the others," Childs says. The one time where their ferocious play almost "got out of hand" was against overmatched Bethune-Cookman College, the very school where Childs would later work for thirty-five years. The Rattlers demolished the Wildcats by a score of 97–0—in the end, they finally held back so as not to go over 100 and complete the humiliation—and Childs's two strongest memories both have to do with the final score more than the game itself.

"When we got back to school some people booed us, saying we should have 'busted the clock,'" he says, explaining that he didn't even know what that meant, but he learned that since the scoreboard couldn't go higher than 99 and would have to go back to 00 if they had kicked a field goal, that was called busting the clock. The other odd thing, he says, is that most people at Bethune-Cookman mistakenly remember the loss as being even worse than it was, repeatedly perpetuating the myth that it was a 99–0 game.

It wasn't until his junior year that Childs, who was more known as a running back than as a defensive back or kick returner, began hearing that he might be pro material. After Childs graduated in 1961, the Boston Patriots of the American Football League drafted him, but his college coach was a good friend of Jim Lee Howell, who put in a good word with the Giants. He signed on as a free agent and spent his first year on their taxi squad, getting to see the legendary team up close in their run to the title game.

"I was in awe of those guys," he says. "I had watched them play on television in high school—Sam Huff and Roosevelt Brown and Rosey Grier and Andy Robustelli and Frank Gifford—and all of a sudden I'm here with them," he says.

And, of course, seeing the home field just about took his breath away. "The first time I walked into Yankee Stadium was awe inspiring," he says, adding that he used to love watching the Yankees take batting practice—especially Roger Maris and Mickey Mantle, who were then locked in their historic race for the single-season home run record. The experience gave him a bit of insight into one overlooked factor as to why the fans often felt Mantle was more deserving of being the one to break Babe Ruth's record: "The ball would come off Mantle's bat loud, like an explosion, and he would hit them out all over the field, but Maris's shots weren't as loud—he would just pull every one down the line and they would just clear the fence."

Away from the stadium, however, the small-town boy never felt quite at home. "New York was a mind-boggling experience," he says, still marveling at things like the concept of alternate-side-of-the-street parking. "Everybody was always running past you at 100 miles per hour."

(In later seasons, Childs would move to Brooklyn, where he felt a little more comfortable and where he maintained his small-town values—he vividly remembers the whole experience of the 1965 blackout, particularly helping a little old lady up to her apartment on the twelfth floor.)

Unfortunately, he then missed the last two years of the Giants' glory days when he was drafted into the Army. He became a military policeman and shipped off to Germany.

"This was during the Berlin crisis and the Cuban missile crisis, and there was a strong threat of nuclear war. We were always told when we traveled to different cities how long that city was expected to last if one country pressed the button," he says. "In Paris and Berlin it was fifteen minutes—that was probably too much information. It was really scary."

Initially, Childs was "very disappointed" about being forced to leave the Giants: "I had a couple of years of my livelihood taken away," he says—and at the time, he didn't even have any way to know that the Giants would reach two more championships while he was gone and then collapse in the year he returned.

But in the end, the Army was a positive experience. "I made friendships that lasted to this day. We have reunions for the Twenty-fourth Infantry football team all over the country; I've gotten to go to San Antonio, San Diego, Atlanta, and other places," he says. "We all bring our wives, children, and even grandchildren."

Additionally, Childs was able to develop his skills as a kick returner while in the Army. His high school and college teams were so dominating that they did all the scoring and didn't receive many kick-offs, but the Army team was not nearly as powerful, and he had plenty of practice at the position where he would eventually make his strongest mark.

Although he carried the ball forty times in his rookie season (and caught eleven passes), Childs spent his career on defense and says he was switched from running back to defensive back by the Giants because of casualties on the defense and because the staff had been wowed by how well he ran in a footrace with known speedster Homer Jones.

But he says head coach Allie Sherman also helped persuade him that the move was in his best interests: "He told me that there was more glory in offense but that I'd last longer on defense and that lots of guys on offense get hurt because they get hit hard on every play," he says. Childs is grateful for that switch since he knows of so many ex-NFLers who have suffered debilitating pain and injuries later in life, "while I can still run and throw and go out and play with my grandchildren."

Of course, Sherman wasn't totally thinking of his player's health, since Childs spent much of his time on both offensive and defensive special teams, or "suicide squads," as they were known back then. "A lot of people didn't want to do that because you were flying downfield and hitting somebody. There were a lot of serious injuries," he says, adding that he came to enjoy the role.

Childs's first season was a disaster for the Giants but his best one offensively—he contributed over 1,200 yards, with 987 of those coming on thirty-four kick returns, including one for 75 yards and one for 100 yards and a touchdown. He was well on his way to setting the Giants' record for kick return yardage. The following season he added two interceptions on the defensive end to his contributions. He was traded after the 1967 season, spending one dismal season in Chicago before quitting in disgust over that organization's disarray.

"I wanted to quit while I was ahead," he says. "I'd seen people who hung around too long."

It was easier for Childs to walk away than for a lot of other players because he was prepared for his post-football life, especially since he had always taken his education so seriously. During off-seasons Childs had returned to Florida, pursuing his master's degree in counseling while working as substitute teacher and helping to coach track as a volunteer at his old high school. (One year, he got a teaching job in nearby Plant City but never told anyone he was still driving back to Lakeland after school to coach—until the day that the two rivals went against each other at a meet in Plant City and all the students came over and told him, "Mr. Childs, you're working for the enemy.")

In 1969, he began working at Bethune-Cookman College and then "time flew by" until he retired as vice president for student affairs, with a boardroom dedicated in his honor. "It really didn't seem like all that long," he says, adding that he never thought about going to a bigger school because he liked the stability this job offered him and his family.

The job did seem to grow in responsibility and complexity over time. He was charged with overseeing "everything outside the classroom," from health services to housing to student activities to Greek life, which—with its tendencies toward drinking and hazing—clearly gave him the most grief. "That was really a job, oh my goodness," he says. "Kids who are smart can really come up with some ideas that would just boggle your mind."

Childs, who lives in Daytona Beach, was going to retire in 2003, but the president of the school asked him to stay on for one more year so they could retire together and the new president could pick his own vice president for student affairs. But the job, which is big enough to really be two or three jobs, was so overwhelming that when Childs finally did retire the following year, his replacement jumped ship after only a few months, and the school came back pleading for Childs to return for one more year.

Childs said no, thanks. He has two children and four grandchildren and his wife, Jesse, who is a retired school principal; he prefers dedicating his days to his family or fishing out on the Gulf or in the Atlantic—one old friend gave him a retirement present of a trip to Aruba, and Childs wasn't about to miss out on that. He also walks around a local mall to stay fit and has been "learning how to wash and iron to help my wife out."

And, of course, Childs still has his mail to answer. Although he was not a major star and he hasn't played for nearly forty years, Childs is astonished to find that he still gets football cards mailed to him regularly from fans seeking autographs—some are now the children and grandchildren of those who once rooted for him. "It's amazing," he says. "I guess if you're a Giants fan, you're a Giants fan for life."

om Costello's first New York Giants contract is framed and hanging in his house. It is proof and an eternal reminder that he defied adversity and overcame the odds, and while the former linebacker is now worth millions, that notion remains a continuing narrative thread running through his life story.

Costello is a New York native, born and raised in Flushing, now a longtime Manhattanite, so playing for the Giants was obviously a great thrill, but it was one he particularly savored because it seemed to have forever slipped beyond his reach.

Costello, whose parents were Irish immigrants, was an all-city football player at Holy Cross, playing wide receiver and defensive back. (He also played baseball against another local Catholic school star by the name of Joe Torre.)

But in Costello's second year of high school, his father, a policeman, died suddenly, a trauma multiplied by the fact that Costello's relationship with his mother was always fraught with issues. "Every day she'd tell me, 'You're not going to make it,'" he says, adding with a laugh that when insomnia forced him into therapy decades later, he told his therapist that his mother's haranguing "made Vince Lombardi look like an amateur act."

For a while, however, it seemed his mother was right. "I had a horrific college experience," Costello says. He earned a scholarship to the University of Virginia but was in over his head; when he failed to properly cite a local newspaper source in a term paper—something he had never really learned about in high school—the professor encouraged two students to accuse Costello of plagiarism. A student court made up of Southern Baptists voted to expel him. "I didn't even know the word 'plagiarism,'" he says, ruefully recalling his naïveté.

He quickly latched on at the University of Miami but got lost in the shuffle among thirteen receivers trying out and was soon on to his third school, the University of Dayton in Ohio, where Giants star Jim Katcavage had gone. The school won only four games in his four years there, and during his senior year a new coach didn't even give him any playing time. Costello was pre-med, preparing for a life as a dentist, but he still obsessed over football, digging out the snow in the dead of winter, then persuading someone to throw passes to him as he ran routes. "My friends would tease me by saying, 'There's a note on your door—Allie Sherman just called and said Kyle Rote is hurt and he needs you,'" Costello recalls.

Costello did enjoy one true thrilling moment when his roommate, Katcavage's younger brother Bob, took the ardent Giants fan with him into the locker room one day when the Giants were playing in Cleveland. Costello still sounds starstruck as he recounts how the older Katcavage shook Costello's hand and said, "Hey, kid, how ya doing?" on his way out; later the two men would become close friends.

But that was a pretty tenuous connection, so after school Costello moved back to Flushing and began applying to dental school. When a friend had asked why he wanted to be a dentist, Costello confessed that it was because the dentist from his neighborhood was the only person who drove a Cadillac—for someone determined to prove himself to his mother, that had a definite appeal, even if the job did not.

Still, Costello couldn't shake the feeling that he wanted to play football, so he began writing letters to semi-pro teams down in West Virginia. Then fate, in the form of his high school coach and mentor Gerry Begley, intervened. Begley still believed his former student had what it took to make it to the pros, and he had the clout to help get him there. "When he said, 'You ought to try out for the Giants,' I said, 'What are you smoking?'" Costello says.

But Begley, a Bronx native, had played at Notre Dame during the Fighting Irish's 1940s heydays and maintained close contact with his former mates, one of whom, Harry Wright, had just been hired as the Giants backfield coach. Begley talked up Costello to Wright, who brought him in to the team's Columbus Circle offices for an interview. All Wright said was that he'd heard great things and so Costello should go talk to head coach Allie Sherman; with Wright vouching for him, Sherman sent Costello directly on down to Wellington Mara's office. When Mara heard that Sherman and Wright had high hopes for the youngster, he pulled out a contract for $8,000 and invited him to training camp.

The Giants signed Costello to be a tight end, but when an opening developed at linebacker, he suddenly found his natural position. He had developed from the 6'1", 165-pound wide receiver of his freshman year to a 6'2", 235-pound strongman, adding 20 pounds of heft just in the final year at Dayton. Looking back, Costello realizes that he was actually lucky to get kicked out of college, because without that delay of one year he never would have filled out enough in time and probably would not have played a down of pro football. "The tragedy became a blessing," he says, an attitude he applies to most of the challenges he has faced in his life.

Costello still gets emotional recalling the night in training camp up in Fairfield, Connecticut, when he found out he had actually made the club. Katcavage said the players would not be going out to the Black Bear that night but would be meeting in one of the players' rooms. When Costello got there, Katcavage, Andy Robustelli, and the other veterans told him, "This is the team."

Costello played in two games in 1964 and eight games in 1965. But the team was collapsing. Sherman, whom Costello describes as "a very good guy" but a terrible coach ruled and ruined by his insecurities, traded or drove out the team's veteran stars. "How the Maras did not name Andy Robustelli as head coach then is beyond me," he says. "That was the biggest mistake they made."

Playing pro football was a dream come true, but Costello soon learned that "even though you're doing something you love, when you're constantly losing, nothing is fun," he says. "It's a different world."

Costello also has harsh words for assistant coach Pop Ivy, whom he calls "the dumbest son of a bitch" and someone threatened by intelligent players. At the start of his third season, Costello intercepted two passes in one exhibition game but was suddenly waived from the Giants the next week. But his mentor Andy Robustelli was coaching the Brooklyn Dodgers of the ill-fated Continental Football League and gave his ex-teammate another chance. Costello's success there led to his signing with the Washington Redskins. But more adversity awaited—Costello injured his back, but coach Otto Graham pressured him to play hurt, leading to a confrontation that bounced Costello from the team ("I told him I thought he was the worst coach in football," Costello says) and back surgery that ended his career.

His football career, that is. Costello, who learned from his frustrating experiences with coaches that he wanted to control his own destiny, not work for corporate bosses, had already been selling insurance in the off-season, making more money than he ever did on the gridiron. Now, he pursued the insurance business full-time, becoming Home Life's top salesman at age thirty and four years later being put in charge of a group of fifty salesmen.

On the surface, Costello had it all: a wife (Mim Fisher, Pete Rozelle's former assistant, introduced to him by Dick Lynch), three kids, a place in Manhattan, and that Cadillac he had dreamed of. But he was working "24/7, totally neurotic, filled with insecurity about money," haunted, it seems, by a conversation he'd had with his mother when he was younger, as an NFL player with $50,000 in the bank. "I said to her, 'Well, you said I'd never make it,'" he recalls, but his triumphant tone was quickly shot down. "And she thought for ten seconds, then said, 'You may have made it, but you'll never keep it.'"

Costello kept pushing himself, doing sales and motivational speaking and even buying a hotel near Port Jervis and opening Tom Costello's All-Sports Camp, in part to give his two brothers an opportunity to get in on the business. "I hated it. It was the most stressful ten years of my life," he says, explaining that although it was successful, it was hard to make money at it and the constant concerns about children's injuries or parents' complaints were unbearable. After he ditched the camp, Costello then briefly dabbled in real estate and still owns some buildings today.

But the biggest change in his life came in 1984 when former Home Life colleague Jim MacDougald broke down in his office, crying because his new consulting career was bombing and he couldn't pay his second mortgage. Costello had just gotten a $350,000 check from a real estate deal, and he turned around and gave his old friend $50,000, saying to get out of consulting and do something that utilized his skills and insights. MacDougald soon created software that could be used to track the newly created COBRA health insurance program for employers.

Costello joined forces on Applied Benefits Research's board of directors with MacDougald, taking a huge risk himself and sticking it out even when failure seemed inevitable. He helped MacDougald raise money to start a company that would implement this program for companies. The company struggled for years, with Costello constantly being forced to round up more money from backers—"those first five years were the most frightening of my life"—before stumbling upon the realization that giant companies like NYNEX were better targets than midsized businesses. The company went public in 1994 and in 1999, right at the peak of the market, Costello persuaded MacDougald and the rest of the board to sell. "I said it's time to go and sit on the beach," he said. And now he can sit all he wants—the company's sale to Ceridian reaped an astonishing $750 million.

Since then Costello has changed his lifestyle. He has worked more at enjoying himself, building golf courses on Long Island, playing golf, spending time with close friends and family—his son just provided him with his first round of grandchildren—and helping those in need.

Sometimes, all those impulses even come together, as in the aftermath of 9/11 when Costello learned that his close friend Dick Lynch's son Richard had died in the Twin Towers. "I never cried like that in my life," Costello says.

The players' friendship had developed when Lynch used to drive Costello from Queens to Yankee Stadium. "I was there for the birth of all of his kids and I sat with him when Richard died," Costello says.

So Costello worked with Lynch to organize an annual charity golf event for Richard's family and others like his, drawing teammates like Frank Gifford, Alex Webster, Harland Svare, and Cliff Livingston as well as more recent Giants like Phil Simms and Mark Bavaro. The event has raised about a million dollars over three years.

"Those are the thrills now," he says. "If you said to me, 'Tom, have I got a deal for you,' I would say, 'Don't even finish the sentence.' I've been blessed. Now I don't need all this materialism anymore."

Tucker Frederickson never made it to veterinary school after all. Growing up in Florida, that had seemed like a natural course of action—his father was a vet, his uncle was a vet, three of his cousins would eventually become vets. In fact, Frederickson, who was an all-American star on his high school football team, chose to journey to Auburn for college over a local school not because of Auburn's pigskin program but because it offered a veterinary school.

At Auburn, however, Frederickson's future took a dramatic turn, one that would lead him to pro football and to New York, where so many doors would open that he'd never look back . . . even after he returned home to Florida. He didn't think about professional football until the middle of his senior year, a season when he would again make all-American. "That's when I said maybe there's a chance."

Frederickson wasn't a huge pro football fan—the Washington Redskins had been the team broadcast down in Florida, but he was more of a college fan. When the Giants called during Thanksgiving weekend of 1964 and said they were going to make him their number one pick, it was "a shocker." The team was picking him ahead of Gale Sayers, who would be taken fourth by the Chicago Bears. Frederickson knew enough to say no, thanks, to Denver when they soon called to offer to make him the number one pick in the upstart American Football League. "I was going to New York," he says. "That was exciting—I had never been to New York before. I had never even seen snow."

The Giants were a team that had just suffered a shocking fall from grace, going from 11-3 and a trip to the title game to a dismal 2-10-2 season. But the turn in the team's fortunes also meant opportunity and a hero's welcome for a young stud from Auburn. He got to start in his second game and never looked back, rushing for 759 yards, eighth best in the league, and five touchdowns on his way to the Pro Bowl as the team managed to achieve a 7-7 record that restored hope to the franchise.

Gregg Browning. Courtesy of Gregg Browning

Sam Huff as a young athlete.
Courtesy of Sam Huff

Sam Huff in his playing days with the Giants. Dan
Rubin photo

Sam Huff at his desk today. Courtesy of
Sam Huff

Bill and Goodrun Austin, late 1950s. Courtesy of Bill Austin

*Bill Austin as a high schooler, mid-1940s.
Courtesy of Bill Austin*

Frank Gifford as a Giant. Dan Rubin photo

Frank Gifford today. Courtesy of Frank Gifford

Clarence Childs in a recent photo. Courtesy of
Clarence Childs

Bill Albright receives a Citizen of the Year award
in 1999. Courtesy of Bill Albright

Brian Kelley. Courtesy of Brian Kelley

Dick Lynch. Courtesy of Dick Lynch

Ernie Koy with his daughter and grandson. Courtesy of Ernie Koy

Jim Clack. Courtesy of Jim Clack

Bill Ellenbogen and family. Courtesy of Bill Ellenbogen

Ron Johnson. Dan Rubin photo

Rosey Grier with some young fans. Dan Rubin photo

Andy Robustelli, Rosey Grier, Dick Modzelewski, and Jim Katcavage. Dan Rubin photo

Homer Jones scores a touchdown at Yankee Stadium. Dan Rubin photo

Alex Webster. Dan Rubin photo

Brad Van Pelt. Dan Rubin photo

Rosey Brown. Dan Rubin photo

Jack Gregory. Dan Rubin photo

Tucker Frederickson and Ernie Koy. Dan Rubin photo

"That whole first year was a good year," he says. "Obviously going to the Pro Bowl as a rookie was a highlight."

Coming off the 1965 year, the team felt confident it had turned the corner, but then Frederickson tore his knee up in an exhibition game and then tried to play on it, only to have it give out on him. "Things were never the same after that," he says. "That was my biggest disappointment—injuries are part of the game, but who knows what could have happened, what would have happened. I felt I was as good as the next guy."

With Frederickson out the whole year, the team collapsed in 1966, finishing 1-12-1. Frederickson came back the next season, but he was never the same player, especially after injuring his other knee in 1967; still, he worked hard whether he was running the ball, blocking, which he was called on to do more after the club acquired Fran Tarkenton as quarterback—in 1970, he had career highs with forty catches and 408 yards receiving—or helping out on special teams, as he did after the club got Ron Johnson to run the ball as Frederickson's career wound down in the early 1970s.

Still, Frederickson says, being a football player in New York made for a magical life, one that put veterinary school far out of his mind. "It was too easy and too much fun. It was just the greatest," he says. "The kind of people you meet, the doors that open."

Frederickson made New York his home and in the off-season in 1967 entered the world of securities and stocks. That made retiring easier when the time came. "I knew what I wanted to do," he says. Frederickson worked for the investment banking firm Allen and Company from 1969 until 1983 on the trading side, handling institutional sales.

But in the early 1980s, married with two kids, Frederickson decided it was time to leave New York. He and his wife Dale moved back to Florida. "I missed the city tremendously at first," he says, but after establishing a hedge fund business, CF Partners, which he ran for four years, he became so busy that he now rarely even comes back. (Events like Wellington Mara's birthday party are a happy exception.) After his third child was born, Frederickson's wife Dale died from brain cancer. He has since remarried, and he and his wife Sherry have a child of their own.

Meanwhile, Frederickson's son Jon Erik is now a wide receiver at Kent State. Frederickson, naturally, refuses to predict a pro future.

"He's just happy to play," he says. "You have to just enjoy your time at each level."

Living in Florida also led to friendships with the likes of Greg Norman and Jack Nicklaus, and soon Frederickson's career had taken another surprising turn—he became a leading golf course developer, working with Norman to create the Medalist Golf Club in Hobe Sound and with Nicklaus to create the prestigious Bear's Club in Jupiter. The golfers lent their insights into the design while Frederickson brought his business savvy and extensive contacts back in New York to help make the business side work.

"It's a ball and one of the big perks is that I get to play at places like the Bear's Club," says Frederickson, who also loves fly-fishing in his spare time. Getting to know such great golfers hasn't helped his game much, he confesses, "but it has helped my pocketbook."

Frederickson has been keeping busy developing a golf course in South Hampton and working with the Ritz-Carlton chain on a joint venture developing golf spas throughout the country. It's a long way from the life of a veterinarian or even a running back, but for Frederickson it is hard to imagine doing anything else. "I like what I'm doing with my life now," he says.

When it comes time for someone to write one of these books about the Green Bay Packers, it's a sure bet that Chuck Mercein will end up in there too—though he only carried the ball thirty-one times in the regular season for the Packers, he made history in the deciding drive of the Ice Bowl, one of the most famous sequences in Super Bowl history. But while that game gave Mercein lasting fame, he's thrilled to have a place in this book on the Giants, the team for whom he played his first two seasons.

"It's like your first love: you never forget," Mercein says. "I'll always be a member of the Giants family."

Not only is he a season ticket holder who attends every Giants home game and raised his son to be a Giants fan, but when it comes time to participate in the Taste of the NFL charity event at the Super Bowl, he works at the Giants booth. (Mercein is involved with nonprofits with the Packers too, sitting on the board of the Vince Lombardi Titletown Legends charity, which serves different needs in Wisconsin.)

Like so many Giants from the mid-1960s, he felt "very hurt and betrayed" by the way Allie Sherman treated him, but he never lost his love and respect for Wellington Mara. In fact, thanks to Mara, all is forgiven with Sherman too—it was Mara who put in a good word for Mercein with former Giants assistant coach Vince Lombardi in 1967, which led to Lombardi's rescuing Mercein from the scrap heap and inserting him into the history books. "It was the best thing that could have happened to me," he says. "And Wellington was instrumental in talking to Coach Lombardi about me and getting me to Green Bay."

Mercein not only won a Super Bowl ring, he got to do it in front of family—he was born in Milwaukee and lived there till he was eleven, and his mother still had numerous relatives in Wisconsin. Mercein was the second of four children, and his father Tom was a local radio and television personality; they moved when he got a drive-time radio gig and another television deal in Chicago. (In

1966, while Mercein was with the Giants, his father would come to New York too, as host of *Milkman's Matinee* on WNEW radio.)

Mercein went to high school in the suburbs there, at New Trier Township High, a school of four thousand with strong academics as well as athletics. Although he had played a bit of junior high school football he says, "I didn't get serious till high school." Still, he soon emerged as a star at linebacker and fullback, being named all-state along with one other Chicago-area fullback, a kid by the name of Dick Butkus. And while Mercein had played basketball and baseball growing up, he soon discovered the shot put in high school, launching one twelve-pound shot over sixty-one feet, breaking the state record by more than three feet. "There were parallels to football—in the shot you needed quickness and strength but especially explosiveness," Mercein says.

Big Ten schools like Michigan, Wisconsin, and Illinois, as well as Ivy League schools like Yale and Princeton, recruited Mercein heavily. Mercein, who says he was thought of as "possible Olympic material" in the shot, seriously considered Stanford, where the track coach, Payton Jordan, was also the Olympic coach. But in the end, Mercein chose Yale, in large part because of Mike Pyle, who grew up down the block from Mercein on Scott Avenue. (At Yale, Mercein moved up to the sixteen-pound shot and reached fifty-eight feet before eventually concentrating more on football.)

"I idolized Mike and wanted to emulate him," Mercein recalls. Pyle, who went on to play center for the 1963 NFL champion Chicago Bears, proved to Mercein that it was possible to go to Yale and make it to the pros, but he also taught Mercein that with this choice "I'd be someone who was not just a football player but a Yale football player."

In retrospect, it was a wise choice, but Mercein says it "was not an easy adjustment." At Yale, he was surrounded by prep school kids, "while when I got there I thought Brown was a color." And he was in a division that didn't allow postseason play, while the Big Ten schools that recruited him were all busy earning Rose Bowl berths during that era. "There were a lot of times I thought, 'Why did I do this?'"

"I might have had a better collegiate and thus a better pro career somewhere else," he says, but ultimately he has no regrets: he shined at fullback, getting named all-East and all-Ivy and attract-

Jack Gregory. Dan Rubin photo

Tucker Frederickson and Ernie Koy. Dan Rubin photo

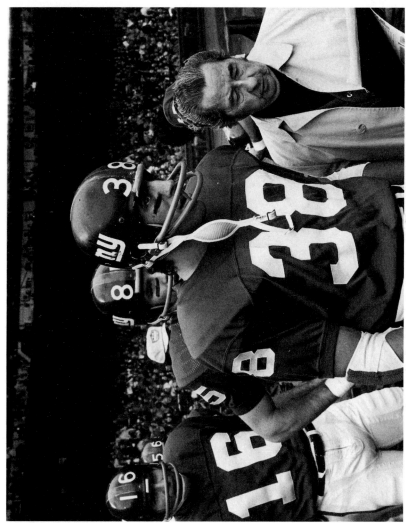

Rob Carpenter and family in 2004. Courtesy of Rob Carpenter

Beasley Reece, NFL analyst. Courtesy of Beasley Reece

Beasley Reece, avid golfer. Courtesy of Beasley Reece

ing the attention of AFL and NFL teams. (He also was a strong kicker, nailing a 48-yard field goal and setting several Yale records.) And Mercein, who has flourished as a Wall Street trader since his playing days, says going to Yale helped him in the rest of his life—he got a strong liberal arts education, majoring in American history and political science, and learned how to write and to think. And in his senior year he was amazed at how the business world of New York flocked to New Haven. "It helped a great deal to be recruited, to have people from all industries coming to our campus," he says.

But the business world would have to wait—the Buffalo Bills of the AFL had drafted him and were offering a three-year guaranteed deal when the Detroit Lions called to say they were interested in making him their number one pick (and the seventh overall). But the Lions backed out when they heard his terms. Then Wellington Mara, who had scouted Mercein, stepped in to match the Bills' offer but with an NFL uniform. Still, Mercein was "very surprised," because the Giants had just made Tucker Frederickson their number one draft pick. "Wellington Mara told me, 'You'll be the fullback and Tucker will be the halfback,' and that's how I thought it was going to be," Mercein says.

So Mercein went off to play in the College All-Star Game in Chicago, thrilled at his first postseason chance—"it was my first opportunity to play with the big boys"—and he stood out, scoring a touchdown and kicking a field goal.

But he also came back with a groin pull, so the Giants started Frederickson off at fullback and relegated Mercein to second string when he returned. But the bigger problem was that coach Allie Sherman seemed to seek out a "contentious" relationship with Mercein. "He seemed to be on me a lot and he always looked at me askance," Mercein says. "He'd say things like, 'Hey, Mercein, we're not playing Harvard this week.'"

Mercein says Sherman—who, he points out, was a "Jewish guy from Brooklyn who had [affected] a Southern accent, and what was that all about?"—seemed to resent the rookie's Ivy League education. "He couldn't have been more wrong. I was not an intellectual or part of the Eastern establishment. I wasn't Andover or Exeter," Mercein says. "I was from the Midwest. The last thing I thought of was myself as being different."

Still, the next season Sherman was forced to play Mercein when Frederickson went down with an injury. Mercein responded with 327 yards rushing and 152 receiving before getting injured again in the second half of the season, when he got a "deep hematoma" in his kidney area.

"Still, the Giants were a terrible team and I had been their leading rusher for six games and felt I had a future there," he says, explaining why he felt so betrayed when it all came to an end the following season when Sherman waived Mercein with minimal explanation one game into the season.

The running back could have just quit and kept his guaranteed money, especially since he was already earning more money each off-season as a trader on Wall Street than he did on the field. But he knew he wasn't done and wanted to show what he could do if he ever got a fair chance, so he went to the minor-league Westchester Bulls and played there, keeping in game shape and hoping for a shot. He contacted Otto Graham, the Washington Redskins coach, whom he had met in Chicago at the All-Star Game after college. "He was my only other contact in the NFL," Mercein recalls. Graham asked Mercein to come down the following Monday to work out and possibly sign with the Redskins.

That Sunday Mercein and his wife packed the car, preparing for the journey from Scarsdale to Washington. That Sunday night they unpacked. In between had come a call from Wellington Mara asking if he'd signed anything with Washington yet and if he'd be "interested in talking to Vince Lombardi." The answer to the first question was "not yet" and the answer to the second question was a hyper-enthusiastic "yes, sir." "The next call you get will be from him," Mara said, explaining that the Packers, hoping for a third straight NFL championship and second straight Super Bowl title, had just lost two running backs, Elijah Pitts and Jim Grabowski, to injuries in one game.

"It was amazing," Mercein says, adding that Lombardi not only gave him a job but also a tremendous "confidence boost—he said, 'You can help us win another world championship.' Coach Lombardi validated my ability to play football."

Mercein carried the ball only fourteen times over the season's final six games, but it gave him a chance to earn the trust of Bart Starr and the other Packers. Before the playoff game against the

Los Angeles Rams in Mercein's hometown at Milwaukee County Stadium, Lombardi told him, "This is why you're here—just do what you're capable of doing and you'll help us win."

"That was tremendous," Mercein remembers. "It was the opposite of how I'd been treated by Allie Sherman."

Mercein responded with a crucial touchdown in the Rams game, but his biggest moment was yet to come. The day of the championship game it was thirteen degrees below zero with a wind chill approaching forty below. Not a great day for playing offense, though for a native Wisconsinite not all that awful. "I was used to cold weather," Mercein says. "We used to go skating on the Milwaukee River and play outside when it was that cold."

And since Jim Grabowski reinjured his knee on the ice that day, Mercein got his chance. With under five minutes to play that day, the Packers got the ball on their own 32-yard line, trailing the Cowboys 17–14. The following 68-yard drive is the kind of march that makes legends out of men like quarterback Bart Starr, but it was the cast-off Mercein who made it all possible, gaining half the yards in the drive.

Mercein's first 7-yard run brought Green Bay a first down. Then, with the clock down to 1:35 and the team on the Dallas 30, Mercein did something unusual in a Packer huddle—he spoke out, telling Starr, who ran the show completely, that he was being left open in the flat. Starr listened and looked, and indeed he found Mercein open. Mercein made a tough adjustment on the pass, grabbed it, and got out of bounds 19 yards later on the 11. Starr rewarded Mercein by calling his number again, running a play called Give 54 that faked a sweep to pull the aggressive Bob Lilly out of position. It worked, and Mercein, who powered through the line, nearly made it to the end zone but got taken down at the 3-yard line.

Donny Anderson failed to get it into the end zone on the next two plays, and the Packers used their last time-out on the 1-yard line with just enough time for one play. Starr then called, "31 Wedge," which was to send two backs ahead of Mercein, who would get the ball and plunge through. But Anderson had nearly fumbled on the icy surface on the previous play, and at the last minute Starr decided to take no chances handing the ball off and instead dove to glory himself, behind the blocking of Jerry Kramer and Ken Bowman, giving the Packers a shocking 21–17 victory.

The famous photo of the play shows Mercein flying forward on the ice behind Starr, his arms raised, not to signal for a touchdown but to show the refs he didn't push Starr into the end zone, which would have been a penalty.

The triumph made Mercein a hero. "To this day I'm still on ESPN and I still get things to sign every week," he says. "To be in the right spot at the right time and to have your shot is what a person wants—then to be able to contribute is just the best feeling."

The Ice Bowl and that drive helped erase Mercein's bitterness toward Sherman and the Giants. "Allie and I are now very friendly," Mercein says. "I don't resent him anymore. After all, he did me the greatest favor in the world—I got a Super Bowl ring and into the history books."

Mercein returned in a backup role in Green Bay the following year but then was dropped during the 1969 season by Lombardi's successor, Phil Bengston. Mercein then followed Lombardi to Washington, but he never saw any action there—the following season Lombardi died and his successor there, Bill Austin (a former Giant), seeking a fresh start, shed the players who had been imported by Lombardi from Green Bay. But then Mercein got two offers, one from the Dallas Cowboys and one from the New York Jets, who had just seen Matt Snell go down with an injury. "I had three kids and a career in New York and I could get to Shea Stadium in twenty minutes," Mercein says. So he chose the Jets, where he played out the year—one of the few decisions he has ever regretted, since he could have played for another contender in Dallas.

Still, the regret is minor. "I had a wonderful career," he says, "and afterwards I was making three times what I ever made playing football." Back when he was twenty-two he had been playing golf when he met an executive at Oppenheimer and Co., who got him a job on the trading desk. Mercein spent ten years there, then moved on to Smith Barney, First Boston, and other companies; today he is a sales trader for Harris Nesbitt, and he still loves the job.

"There are obvious parallels to football," he says. "There's a lot of down time but then there's real excitement when that bell goes off. There's the instant gratification: you don't have to wait three months to find out if you made a successful transaction, you can often find out in five minutes."

"There are a lot of ups and downs and you can learn valuable lessons from the downs. I learned the most valuable a long time ago, of course—to never give up. And if you have a good day or bad day, the next day the bell will go off again and it's another ball game."

There was only one day for Mercein that he will never shake off, and that, of course, is 9/11. In that he is more a typical New Yorker than an ex-NFLer. Mercein, who has four grown children from his first marriage and eleven grandchildren, was living with his second wife, Jody, in Battery Park City. "It was the most beautiful place, one of the greatest neighborhoods with the river and the esplanade, and those two buildings looming made it like living in a canyon."

That morning, Mercein was at work in his Times Square office, chatting on the phone with a trader he knew named Artie Simon. Mercein had recently given Simon, a Packers fan, a Lombardi lithograph he'd had autographed by his former Green Bay teammates. They hung up the phone. Mercein glanced at the television and saw the image of the plane smashing into the World Trade Center. Artie Simon worked in one of those towers. Mercein tried calling back, but the line was dead. Simon did not get out.

But Mercein had another, more immediate worry. His wife—who had been on the 105th floor of one tower during the 1993 bombing—worked as a personal trainer for Cantor Fitzgerald, and Mercein didn't know exactly where she was. "I couldn't find her for hours," he says. "There was no communication. I was paralyzed with fear. I literally thought I'd have a heart attack at my desk. That was the worst day of my life."

Jody was fine; she was actually three blocks away at the time and had walked uptown with the fleeing throngs, but the couple knew literally hundreds of people who died that day, including some of their closest friends. "It was just horrifying," Mercein says. "It was the greatest tragedy and most seminal event of our lives. I think about those people every day and I always will."

The first weekend after the attack the couple went, escorted by armed guards, back into their Battery Park City apartment to retrieve some valuables. But they could not live there anymore. They stayed briefly in Darien with Mercein's son Tommy and then eventually settled in a townhouse in White Plains. They have not gone back to the site, and Mercein says he doesn't know how he would have handled returning to work if his job was anywhere downtown.

If there's anything positive in the aftermath for Mercein, it's that the event has made him "realize how precious life is. I have always been a pretty grateful person all my life, but now even more I feel blessed and live every day with that feeling."

E rnie Koy ended up right back where he started. Sure, he enjoyed his years in the NFL, living in New York, doing a little bit of everything for the Giants—running, receiving, returning kicks, and even punting—but, as a good witch once taught, "There's no place like home."

Home for Koy—for many athletically gifted Koys, in fact—is the tiny town of Bellville, Texas. The town could practically be re-named Koyville. Now, Ernie wasn't the first Koy to venture north to the big city to play a little pro ball. His dad, also Ernie Koy, helped form the football team at nearby Sealy High School, then went on to become a legend at the University of Texas before sign-ing with the New York Yankees. (During the off-season he met his future wife, Jane, at a dance in Bellville, and in 1936 they were married there.)

The Yankees traded him to the Brooklyn Dodgers—Koy would play five years in the bigs, but none more memorable than that first year in Brooklyn. He homered his first time up and finished among the league leaders in doubles, triples, and steals, but more impor-tantly he earned a footnote in history. Koy was the second-to-last out in Johnny Vander Meer's historic second straight no-hitter (in baseball's first night game). But Koy had one notable success that night—in a stunt before the game, he raced against legendary sprinter Jesse Owens, and, with an 8- or 10-yard head start (ac-counts vary), the fastest man in baseball actually beat the Olympic champ in the 100-yard dash.

After four years in the Navy during World War II, Ernie Koy Sr. and his wife, Jane, came to Bellville and bought Cameron's Store, the local five-and-ten, from Jane's parents. They lived a block away, and Ernie Jr. would help sweep out the store before school. Ernie Jr. starred in football, baseball, and track in Bellville, and his brother Ted later followed in his footsteps. Their sister Margaret played basketball at Bellville and covered the football games as sports editor for the local paper while still in school. High school football, of course, was the most important of those sports, the heart and soul of a small Texas town. In 1960 the Brahmas made it to the 2A title game against Denver City, a regional powerhouse. "We chartered a train for two thousand people, which is about how many people we had in the town," Koy recalls. "They delayed one funeral and left one cop behind and everyone came to the game." (The fact that they lost only by 26–21 to their heavily favored foe was considered cause for celebration.)

Playing for crowds of family and friends like that, Koy says, would later make playing for fifty thousand anonymous faces seem free of pressure. Koy says his father never forgot his heady days in New York. "In 1957, after they'd learned the Dodgers were leaving, Mother and Daddy wanted us to see Ebbets Field, so they took us up to see a ball game," Koy says, adding that through his connections, the family even got into the Dodgers' locker room. "That was a big thrill."

But Koy's father also emphasized that education had to come before football. 'He'd say that when you were through with football you wouldn't be able to peel it and eat it," Koy laughs.

Both Koy brothers went, like their dad, to the University of Texas (UT), and both played for national championship teams there before heading up to New York. (Ted was on the 1969 UT team and then ended up in Buffalo with the Bills; Margaret went on to cover high school football in Abilene and is believed to be the first woman sportswriter on a daily newspaper in Texas.)

Ernie was there for the national championship team in 1963, which topped Roger Staubach's team 28–6 in the Cotton Bowl, and he led the team in rushing in 1964 and almost helped lead the team back to the top. The team's only loss was against Arkansas, which came after Koy scored near the game's end to make it 14–13; the coach went for a two-point conversion (there was no overtime then) and failed. In the Orange Bowl, Koy gained national attention when he ran 79 yards for a touchdown on the game's second play against Joe Namath's Alabama. Koy finished the day with 133 yards and two touchdowns, but while Texas's 21–17 win knocked Alabama from the top, it handed the number one ranking to undefeated Arkansas.

Both the Giants and the Houston Oilers of the American Football League (AFL), which was then in the midst of a bidding war with the NFL, drafted Koy. (Namath, of course, would go to the Jets in the AFL.) Houston was close to home, but Koy felt the pull of the big time, of the NFL, and of New York, where his father had played. Additionally, he says, so many of his teammates were going to New York for the Jets or Giants that he knew he wouldn't be the only "country boy."

Still, "New York was a shock," he says, remembering that in his rookie year he shared a Long Island apartment with three teammates, but when they returned from their first road game, they could not find the building and spent an entire night driving around. Several years later he watched two rookies, "big ol' boys, looking at all the tall buildings, standing with their mouths open so wide their tonsils were going to get sunburned," and he knew that he had adjusted to life in New York.

Koy was part of a group called the Baby Bulls, a bunch of promising young backs that the Giants hoped would turn the team back around. The others were Tucker Frederickson, Steve Thurlow, Ernie Wheelwright, Chuck Mercein, and Smith Reed. Koy made a favorable impression coming off the bench at halfback his rookie season, averaging 5.0 yards on thirty-five carries, but he contributed significantly on special teams, punting fifty-five times for an impressive 41.2 yard average while returning twenty-one kicks and averaging 19.1 yards per try.

"The more you could do, the more valuable you were," Koy says. "I was just glad to get the chance."

The next year Koy saw a bit more action, but it was an utter disaster for the Giants—the team was so decimated by injuries that at one point management told Koy he should be ready to stand in as an emergency quarterback.

"It was really rough. We had a number of quarterbacks and everyone got hurt. We lost more games that year than I had in all my games in high school and college put together. It was a hard year emotionally."

By contrast, the 1967 season was his happiest and most fulfilling one in New York. The addition of Fran Tarkenton not only settled the situation at quarterback and made the Giants at least competitive, it also fit in well with Koy's talents. "Fran was a breath of fresh air," he says, with his scrambling and looking for any open receiver. "I could swing out of the backfield and catch the ball—I had played baseball, so I could catch."

As a result, he produced nearly 1,000 yards of offense, rushing 146 times for 704 yards and catching thirty-two passes for 212 yards more, while still serving as the team punter.

Koy had two more respectable seasons, although he was used less frequently as nagging injuries increasingly slowed him— playing on converted baseball fields that were poorly maintained for football took its toll. Finally, in 1970, he was barely able to play at all. "I felt I had a couple of years left, but the injuries had piled up and I had gone over the hill," he says.

Koy had served in the National Guard during one off-season and worked for Allied Chemical a couple of times, but when his career was over, he knew where he was heading. Koy had just been married in 1970, and his wife, Barbara, was from Queens, but Koy says he thought about staying in New York "for five seconds. Then I got my pickup and loaded up her stuff and started south. Her mother was standing on one side of her and her sister was on the other and I said, 'Let's go.' And they said, 'Just like that, you're going?' And I said, 'Just like that.'"

Koy would return to New York for another athletic venture in the 1990s, when he started running marathons. He originally began jogging because "after I got through playing, my appetite was still there but my activity had stopped and, with young children, the only time I had where I could do anything was early in the morning."

He and some friends began jogging, then doing 5K and 10K races, until in 1989 someone decided they should try a marathon. They ran the one in Houston, and in the 1990s Koy returned twice to New York to conquer the famous race in his old stomping grounds. "I got to see more of the city and all its neighborhoods than I ever did when I was with the Giants," he says. "I really enjoyed it."

Koy's old high school coach invited him to Sam Houston State College in Huntsville, where he could help coach football while earning the master's degree he would need to go into banking back in Bellville and where Barbara could get a teaching certificate. In 1974, with that accomplished, the Koys returned to Bellville, where his sister Margaret also was living. Under the proud eye of Ernie Sr., her son played football for Bellville and later Harvard, while Ernie Jr.'s kids also played at Bellville—Robert went on to be quarterback at the University of Texas, Andy was a guard who later went to the Naval Academy and did the shot and discus there, daughter Lucy starred in volleyball and softball, then went to UT (and lives in town), while the youngest, Jess, was a running back like his dad and then went to Sam Houston to study to become a banker. (Ernie's brother Ted became a vet and ended up two hours away in Georgetown, but one daughter also went to the University of Texas, while the other was also an athlete, playing basketball at Rice.)

Meanwhile, Koy still goes to work every day at the bank—across the street from the hospital where he and his siblings and his children were all born. But the bank expanded in 1980, buying up the site next door, which was, in fact, his family's old five-and-dime store. So now Koy's office is where his parents used to have their cash register. His wife keeps busy teaching Spanish to pre-K children.

"I feel proud not just about the sports but because I feel maybe we helped the town too," he says.

The Roller Coaster Era

As summer turned to fall in 1970, one member of the New York Giants was paying careful attention to the American League batting race between California's Alex Johnson and Boston's Carl Yazstremski. When Johnson edged out Yaz by mere percentage points, that Giant felt tremendously proud. And then Ron Johnson returned to chasing Washington's Larry Brown for title of NFL rushing leader.

Johnson never caught Brown, but his 1,027 yards gained were the catalyst for the Giants that year—right in the middle of the worst stretch in Giants history, Johnson provided a bright spot, a season of hope. "It was wonderful, just an unbelievable year," says the team's first-ever 1,000-yard rusher. "The teamwork was amazing—we all melded together."

(With his 487 yards receiving, Johnson actually did lead the league in offense from the line of scrimmage, a fact that was a pleasant surprise to him when he learned it nearly thirty-five years later.)

Although the team would soon lapse back into its bumbling ways and although Johnson would have only two more fully healthy seasons, his dazzling performance in 1970 forever earned him a special place in the hearts of long-suffering Giant fans.

Johnson grew up in Detroit, the youngest of five children in a close-knit family. "Candidly, as the baby I was spoiled." Alex was five years older, so he was "more of an idol than a rival," Johnson recalls. In fact, one of Johnson's fondest memories is of hearing Alex's proud voice on the phone after Ron had set a college rushing record with 347 yards. "He said Johnny Bench had told him about it and he was just so happy for me—he was just over the top with joy."

Having an older brother like Alex also gave Ron insight into the athlete's life. He was there when Michigan State told Alex he could not play both football and baseball, with Alex then choosing to turn pro, and Ron spent several summers hanging out with Alex as he journeyed through the minors.

Ron says he was "a pretty damn good baseball player too"—there was more organized baseball than football when he was little—but he decided he wanted to go to college, so after the age of fifteen, "football just took over my life."

Despite his brother's experience, Michigan State was initially Johnson's first choice "because they had a more consistent football program and because it was more of a party school than the University of Michigan."

But the coaching staff at Northwestern High School pushed him toward the University of Michigan because of its academic reputation. And Johnson soon found that Michigan was indeed the one place that took him seriously.

"I was a proud young African-American and I wanted to study engineering, but most schools I would visit would say, 'Maybe you need to go into phys ed,'" Johnson says. He really was interested in both business and engineering, but he knew that he could start in engineering and switch over to business but that playing catch-up in engineering would be impossible. And while schools might have viewed all athletes in that patronizing manner regardless of race, Johnson saw it differently. "I took it as an African-American being pushed in that direction."

By contrast, Johnson recalls, Michigan coach Bump Elliott said, "Let's go over to the engineering school and I'll introduce you to the dean." Additionally, he was impressed by Elliott's honesty—"Every other school told me I'd start as a sophomore to get me to go there, but Bump said, 'Ron, you won't start till your junior year.'"

Johnson felt that Elliott was a coach he would respect, so he signed on. When he got to school he learned two things pretty quickly: "I discovered girls and I found that my roommate would go to sleep at 11 p.m. and I'd be up at 2 a.m. trying to keep up with my work."

But he did not trade his engineering major for phys ed, instead switching over in his junior year to a business major. That was the year, of course, that football would take even more time, as he did indeed get his shot at starting. Johnson gained over 1,000 yards, but he also gained valuable confidence because the team got to work out with members of the Detroit Lions. "They were absolutely wonderful and nurturing to us," he says, adding that seeing that he could catch passes from Earl Morrall had him suddenly believing that a career in the NFL was a possibility.

Then came 1968, and the NFL suddenly seemed a certainty. Johnson set school and conference records with 1,391 yards and nineteen touchdowns while winning the Big Ten's Most Valuable Player award. His year was highlighted by two events—the astonishing 347 yards gained against Wisconsin and the day he was named captain of the Michigan team.

Most teams had at least one offensive and one defensive captain, but that year Michigan went with just Johnson, who was also their first ever African-American captain. Johnson points out that he was one of only twelve minorities out of fifty players, meaning that he had the support of all the white players, which was particularly noteworthy in 1968, when American cities like Detroit were being torn apart by racial rioting.

"It was the biggest honor I ever had in football," he says. "And the older I get, the more special that becomes to me. It makes me feel so proud that we got past the racial issue."

Johnson was drafted by Cleveland and went through a rough rookie season, a definite comedown from the tremendous finish to his college career. Although he had starred at halfback and tailback, the Browns wanted to make him a fullback, blocking for their perennial Pro Bowler Leroy Kelly. But Kelly got hurt in the first game and Johnson stepped in, rushing for 119 yards. After four games Johnson was second in the league in rushing and thought he'd earned a share of the football. "But then Kelly came back and I didn't get to carry the ball at all anymore," he says.

The coaching staff promised they'd sit down and talk after the season, but instead the Browns shocked him by shipping him out to New York. After getting over his initial disappointment, Johnson realized "it was the best thing that ever happened to me. The Giants did not have a featured back, so it was a great opportunity."

Johnson seized the opportunity in 1979, with 263 rushes and forty-eight receptions for a total of 1,514 yards and twelve touchdowns. The Giants posted a surprising 9-5 record under second-year coach Alex Webster, remaining in the playoff hunt until the season's final day.

Johnson was almost too central to the team—the next year he badly injured his leg playing basketball in the off-season, then came back too soon to the Giants and tore cartilage in his knee. He played in only two games and the Giants won only four the whole season. Johnson bounced back in 1972 with another Pro Bowl season, gaining 1,182 yards rushing and 451 receiving while tying for the NFL lead with fourteen touchdowns. But while Johnson led the team to a respectable 8-6 record, the easygoing Webster was having trouble controlling the players, and the team was on the verge of collapse again.

"Alex was a great guy to play for, a player's coach, but it was like he was one of us," Johnson says, recalling a road trip when he and Bob Tucker returned to the hotel at 10:30 for an 11 p.m. curfew only to have Webster insist they join him and Joe Walton for drinks. "At midnight we said, 'Alex, we have to go to bed,' but he said, 'Have another drink.'"

Johnson says that the 1970 team had dedicated, hardworking veterans who knew their limits and who felt they had "something to prove" on the field but that the newer personnel later saw Webster merely as someone they could take advantage of. "Those guys didn't give 100 percent and really ruined the team," Johnson says.

Johnson gained nearly 1,200 total yards in 1973, but the team won only two games; slowed by injuries, Johnson was reduced to a part-time contributor in his final two seasons as the Giants continued to wallow as one of football's worst teams. In 1976 he headed to Dallas, joining the perennial powerhouse only to hurt his knee in an exhibition game. "After my first knee operation I had made a promise to myself that if I ever needed another one, I'd know it was time to go home," he says.

But home was no longer Michigan—Johnson had settled in quite nicely in New Jersey and had been working for Dean Witter on Wall Street in the off-season for three years. "My wife, Karen, is from the Detroit area also, but she established her own fashion and interior design business and she once said, 'If you ever leave here, you'll be going without me,'" he says, explaining that the one time it came up was when ABC—for whom he had done some work—offered him full-time college football broadcasting jobs in either Maryland or Wisconsin.

After retiring, Johnson, who now lives in Summit, joined up full-time with Dean Witter, selling institutional municipal bonds to banks and insurance companies. While he liked the work, he soon found himself frustrated by the same old jock stereotypes he had faced after high school. Johnson says that to be successful in that field, a salesperson needs to work closely with the traders, "but they treated me like an athlete who should just be happy to be there, sitting around," he says. "That burned me up. I wanted to work hard. There were people making fortunes down there."

So Johnson left Dean Witter to work in sales for the textile company Burlington Industries. But he'd always wanted to fend for himself, to run his own business—he had been about to buy three McDonald's franchises in Cleveland when he was traded to New York—and when his wife got pregnant he knew "if I didn't start it right then I would never do it. So I jumped on into that world."

Johnson researched his investment possibilities and settled on Kentucky Fried Chicken. "When I first started, I had to find a site and build my own restaurant and I'd add a new one about every year and a half, but in the mid-nineties KFC decided they didn't want to run the restaurants anymore, so they started selling blocks of them," says Johnson.

He snapped up a half-dozen in Tennessee and in 1998 he purchased another six, this time back home in Michigan; today he has twenty-four franchises, "the more the better." While the travel sometimes "gets a little old," the trips to Michigan are usually a pleasure, visiting his family and friends as well as his alma mater.

Meanwhile, Johnson has continually challenged himself in other ways—in the 1980s, he earned a master's in business administration from Fairleigh Dickinson University. While the emphasis on marketing was helpful to his new business, it wasn't the motivation. "It was about my own internal drive—I had always wanted an MBA and that was the time to do it," he says.

He also served on the boards of trustees for the Sports Hall of Fame of New Jersey and the University of Michigan and is on his way to becoming chairman of the National Football Foundation College Hall of Fame. He has also been involved with Big Brother and other grassroots organizations, but he says, "I got tired of going to meetings and not being interactive with people, not doing the things I wanted to do."

After the infamous Central Park "wilding" incident of 1989, Johnson decided the time had come to take "hands-on" action, and he found two like-minded former Giants in Terry Jackson and

George Martin. Together they formed Minority Action Network, or MAN Etc., Inc., a nonprofit group dedicated to helping urban youth in the tri-state area. Other former Giants like Harry Carson and Zeke Mowatt have since gotten involved with the group, which has given out nearly $500,000 in scholarships to nearly two hundred students with a complementary mentoring program since its birth. It has also been involved with helping to run an SAT prep program for athletes and a work-cooperative program in Paterson, a Young Fathers Program in Newark, the Harlem Junior Tennis Program, and the African-American History Program at Fairleigh Dickinson. They've even expanded to add serving Thanksgiving dinners to seniors and the homeless in Patterson and other towns—Johnson himself gets most of the food donated from his KFC suppliers.

"This is really important to me," he says. "My coaches in high school taught us a lot about life—they taught us that you never forget where you come from and that you give something back."

H e wasn't particularly quick. He didn't come out of a big football program. He didn't even make it to the NFL in his first try. But once Bob Tucker landed in New York, he immediately made his mark, helping the Giants briefly elevate their play, averaging fifty-one pass receptions for 709 yards over his first four seasons.

Growing up in the small town of Hazleton, Pennsylvania, Tucker played everything from running back to defensive back in junior high school. But when he went out for the high school team as a sophomore, "the coach shoved a ball in my gut and said, 'Go play center.'" Tucker, who also played defensive tackle, wasn't thrilled with the assignment, but it turned out to be a fortuitous one. The line coach, Jim Tricolli, was "excellent in demonstrating the fundamentals of blocking."

Those fundamentals would serve him well when he was shifted over after arriving at tiny Bloomsburg University. "The coach there said, 'We have seven centers—can't you play somewhere else?'" Tucker recalls. Since he'd always wanted to be an offensive weapon, he quickly replied, "Sure, tight end."

What he soon learned was that tight end was a unique position—you have to be fleet and have good hands on the pass plays, but you also have to be an offensive lineman on the running plays. "You can't catch enough passes to cover any ineptitude in the blocking," he says, "but in coaching everyone can tell you who to block, but most can't tell you how to block."

Tucker watched games on television to study how other tight ends ran their routes, although he adds that he later learned a great deal from Giants offensive coach Joe Walton. A three-time all-conference player who set nine school records and once caught 290 yards' worth of passes in a game, Tucker was studying biology and chemistry and planned to go into teaching.

After college Tucker got invited to the Boston Patriots training camp . . . along with about 120 other hopefuls. "I came in as a really raw tight end and lasted till the final cut," he says, although he was mostly stuck on special teams and not given a chance to prove himself. The club offered him a spot on the taxi squad, but the money wasn't enough, so instead he opted for a teaching job at Acton-Boxborough Regional High School and a spot on the Lowell Giants, the Patriots' farm team in the Atlantic Coast Football League (ACFL). (Other NFL teams had affiliations with ACFL teams in places like Hartford, Harrisburg, and Roanoke.)

Tucker taught during the day, coached junior varsity football in the afternoon, and then drove from Acton to Lowell at night for practice; the team's games were on weekends. Tucker, who connected well with quarterback Jim Cochran, impressed everyone by leading the league in receiving, which earned him an invitation back to training camp from Patriots coach Mike Holovak. So Tucker kept teaching, awaiting the new season. Then he got a call inviting him to the Philadelphia Eagles' training camp along with an offer to otherwise play for their farm team in Pennsylvania, the Pottstown Firebirds. Cochran had already headed that way, but Tucker said no, thanks, he had a shot with the Patriots. Then he learned that Holovak had been fired and new coach Clive Rush literally responded to his call by saying, "Bob who?" So it was off to Philly, where he was again shunted off to special teams then offered only a taxi squad position.

"I was too good to get cut, but because I was a free agent they were afraid to take a chance and really play me," Tucker says. This time he accepted. He lived in Pottstown, drove to Philly for practices during the day, then, since taxi squad players could play on the farm teams, drove back and practiced with the Firebirds at night. For the second straight year he led the league in receiving, and Pottstown won the championship. Although he was technically property of Philadelphia, after the season ended he got an invitation to meet with Green Bay and then with Chicago and New York. He signed with the Giants, but while the Firebirds gave him their blessing, the Eagles told him he had to come back to Philadelphia. He refused and ultimately got his way, which was fortunate for the Giants—who needed a tight end—and for Giants fans, who needed someone who could help the floundering franchise.

Part of the problem was that Wellington Mara's loyalty—which is what endeared him to so many players—is also what ultimately undermined the team, Tucker says. "There would be veteran players on the bench because Wellington didn't have the heart to cut them, but their best years were behind them and it stopped young players from developing," he says, adding that until the arrival of George Young, the front office and scouting department were simply places where old Giants went to live out their lives, regardless of competence.

But Tucker made his mark in his first season in 1970, when he caught forty passes for 571 yards and scored five touchdowns, and the Giants rolled to a 9-5 record, their best season since 1963. "Fran Tarkenton was smart as hell and a real general out there—he would just pick, pick, pick at the other team's defense," Tucker recalls, adding that the problem at that point was that the Giants defense couldn't stop anybody. (Indeed, in 1970 the team finished eighth in points scored but only fourteenth in points allowed, and in two of the following three years they'd have the league's second-worst defense.)

The following year the team, beset by injuries to key players like Ron Johnson, stumbled, but Tucker upped his totals to fifty-nine passes for 791 yards. In 1972, the Giants bounced back to 8-6 and Tucker had his best year ever—he caught fifty-five passes for 794 yards and was named all-pro.

But soon the team started collapsing. Coach Alex Webster was replaced by the defensive-minded Bill Arnsparger, and Fran Tarkenton went back to Minnesota; the Giants collapsed—in 1974 they scored the fourth fewest points of any team—and Tucker's numbers went into a downward spiral: from 1974 through 1976 he averaged only thirty-nine catches for 493 yards.

"Arnsparger dismantled the offense and defense and he wanted to coach everything," Tucker says. While he believes Arnsparger was a great defensive coach whose overall emphasis and hiring of Marty Schottenheimer were ultimately the first building blocks to the team's revival in the 1980s, his offensive thinking was "hurry up and punt so I can get my defense back out—he once even sent in a call for a quick kick on third and long. We became a drab, meaningless entity."

Tucker saw Arnsparger as surrounded by yes-men who were equally inept offensively and was further dismayed when the coach was replaced by John McVay, who came straight from the World Football League and brought with him his staff and players.

"It was abysmal—the coaches were unprofessional," he says, adding that he became so disgruntled and complained loudly enough that he eventually forced a trade to Minnesota.

Although Tucker feels regret about not having played his whole career with the New York organization, he says arriving in Minnesota "was like I'd died and gone to heaven. I was back in the football business."

Indeed, although because he came over in midseason he essentially backed up Stu Voigt while learning the Vikings system, he was reunited with Tarkenton on a team led by the esteemed Bud Grant, and he got to taste the playoffs as the Vikings made it back to the NFC championship. "It was thrilling," he says. "The Giants had been so bush league." In 1978, he bounced all the way back with forty-seven catches and 540 yards—his best numbers since 1973—nearly becoming one of five Vikings with at least fifty receptions. Then Tarkenton and many of the other Vikings veterans began retiring, and the team foundered a bit while Tucker's role was reduced over his final two years.

Tucker was interested in coaching, but there were no opportunities in Minnesota, and given the "cloud I'd created in New York so I could get away it wasn't feasible to go back and knock on the door and say, 'Look who's here.'"

So he moved back to Pennsylvania and went to work for a local footwear company in the marketing and sales division for many years until the company went out of business. At that time the issue of solid waste disposal was becoming controversial in and around his hometown of Hazleton, so Tucker, whose college years studying science made it easy for him to grasp everything from the subsurface studies to the hydrology issues, got involved with a company trying to design a new facility to handle the material. "It was mostly innocuous material—construction debris and things like that," he says, "and this was an old coal mining area where the land had been desecrated, so I said let's reclaim the land and turn it back into an asset."

Unfortunately, years of illegal dumping by other outfits had residents believing horror stories that there might again be trucks opening their valves and dumping right into the mines or even nuclear materials dumped there. "We just couldn't convince people and we never got the zoning changed," he says.

Still, Tucker's planning there caught the attention of businesses in New York, and he ended up running a construction and demolition business and at one point serving as president of a company called Phoenix Disposal, a hazardous waste hauling subsidiary, although the shift in emphasis to garbage disposal ultimately led Tucker to sell the business and change careers yet again. In recent years he has been working for an old friend who runs the ninety-year-old family-run Port Morris Marble and Tile Company, which is involved with much of the marble and tile installation, maintenance, and renovation in the city.

Tucker, who is involved with the renovation side of the business, says he enjoys the challenge of learning something new. "It's a very interesting field and it takes a lot of experience—there are fifteen ways to clean something but fourteen of them might be wrong, depending on the type of marble or tile."

Although he still lives in Hazelton, Tucker keeps a place near Giants Stadium so he doesn't have to commute during the week. But now that his kids have graduated from college and he has fewer financial obligations and he need not be tied to one place, he's also thinking of pursuing another new challenge—finding a way to return to the game he loves. "Now that I'm freed up, I've started to think about getting into coaching," he says. "I could afford to start as an assistant coach somewhere—even though it wouldn't be a lot of money, I think it would be fun."

These days it's no big deal for a star player to jump from one team to another in search of a bigger payday, but back in 1972 when Jack Gregory played out his option year with the Cleveland Browns it was virtually unheard of. But the Browns' loss was clearly the Giants' gain—the defensive end was a crucial building block to a stellar defensive unit that was one of the few bright spots for the team between 1963 and 1981.

The Giants were especially lucky because Gregory ultimately would have preferred staying in Cleveland but got caught in a power game in Cleveland's front offices. "I really didn't want to leave," he says, "but things got out of hand."

"Things" were the negotiations: Gregory had caught the attention of Mark McCormack and IMG, the burgeoning sports agency. He had been paid $27,000 in the final year of his contract, but his agent, Ed Keating, wanted $35,000 for the following season. The Browns, under new coach Nick Skorich, countered with an offer of $33,000. Clearly it was not a huge discrepancy. But, Gregory says, instead of the player negotiating with owner Art Modell, with whom he'd had a good relationship, it was his agent and his coach dissecting the deal. "I got caught in the middle," Gregory says.

And so the relationship deteriorated and Gregory played out his option in 1971, becoming one of football's first free agents. He says the Browns and the league tried making an example of him: "They saw me as a rabble-rouser and blackballed me. They wouldn't let me go to any team with a winning record," he says. "My choices were Atlanta, Philadelphia, New Orleans, and New York."

He chose the Giants because they offered a three-year, $150,000 deal—he then went out and made it back to the Pro Bowl twice as a Giant; he was the captain of the defense for five years and was among the league's sack leaders and most durable players.

All in all, a pretty good run for someone who says he always approached the game with a sort of clinical detachment, viewing it as a job. "I don't even know if I enjoyed football—it was just what I did," he says. But it was not just a job; in fact, it was the family business: although he earned the nickname "Big Jack" in the NFL, he was following the footsteps of his father, also named Jack, who had played guard for the Cleveland Browns in the 1940s.

Jack Sr. encouraged his son to lift weights and be athletic but never pushed his son into football, yet Jack Jr. says, "I never had any doubt in my mind that I was going to play pro football."

Born Earl Jackson Gregory Jr. in Tupelo, Mississippi, Gregory was raised in small-town Okolona, where he played football, basketball, and track in high school—he won the shot put in his senior year at the conference finals and finished fourth in the state. "We only had twenty seniors and I sure didn't play in the band," he says, explaining why he was involved in every sport.

In football he had played wide receiver—he was only 185 pounds at graduation—and he went off to the University of Chattanooga to play tight end and defensive end as a lanky kid looking to find a role. "They didn't even have a weight room there. I had to join a health studio to work out," Gregory says. But he bulked up to 235 pounds by the end of his time there, playing tight end and defensive end and earning honorable mention for all-American in 1965, his third year. Although he wasn't a senior, Gregory was drafted in the ninth round of a special "future" draft by the Cleveland Browns and by the AFL's Buffalo Bills. He thought about turning pro and left school during the semester, going home to his family's farm to chop wood and ponder his future. Buffalo coach Lou Saban called asking if he could fly Gregory up to Buffalo, but Gregory also got a call from local boy made good, Bookie Bolin—the Giants guard warned him that he had been caught in a similar situation and had lost his last year of eligibility. So Gregory didn't go to Buffalo and also didn't go back to Chattanooga, instead transferring to Delta State, which had just adopted a wide-open offense. He caught fifty-one passes and set a school record by gaining 557 yards; he also filled in at linebacker due to injuries, while winning the shot put at the 1966 Southwestern Invitational Track Meet.

Then it was time for the pros, and this time Gregory chose Cleveland because he wanted to prove himself. "I had a bunch of buddies from home who went to Ole Miss and said that I wasn't good enough to play there, so I wanted to make sure I went to the NFL and proved myself with the best, which I couldn't do in Buffalo," he says.

Gregory thought of himself as equally adept and comfortable on offense and defense, but upon arriving in the pros he made the permanent move to defense, in part because tight ends tend to have shorter careers and in part because the Browns had young tight ends but veteran defensive linemen so he thought he'd get an opportunity quicker on the defensive side of the ball. "It was a better opportunity for me," he says, adding that he learned his technique by watching game films. "My first coach in the NFL, Blanton Collier, told me to watch the films and develop my own personal style. So I started keeping a notebook, watching the offensive tackles and figuring out what I could."

He figured out plenty: the 6'5", 250-pound end was a starter in his third year, a Pro Bowler in 1969, and the Browns' defensive player of the year the following season; he also gained notoriety when he sacked Joe Namath in the very first *Monday Night Football* game ever in 1970.

Gregory was keeping plenty busy in the off-season too. He would show up late to the Browns' (and later the Giants') summer camp every year because from 1967 to 1973 he served in the Mississippi National Guard at Camp Shelby, in the 223rd Engineering Battalion, Company C.

"Art Modell was really good about it—they flew me into Tupelo once on a Lear jet and picked me up on Sunday," says Gregory, who also visited Vietnam on a USO tour in February 1972. "It was my obligation and I'm certainly glad I did it."

Gregory also worked as an auctioneer at established companies like the Yokley & Lundy Auction Company before founding his own company, the Rebel Auction Company. And after his son EJ was born extremely prematurely, Gregory also devoted time each year beginning in 1975 to Easter Seals, helping with their annual telethon for two decades, serving on their board of directors, and hosting and organizing the Jack Gregory Easter Seal Rodeo from 1978 to 1984. (EJ was plagued by respiratory problems as a boy but grew up to work in politics and is now in investment banking.)

In between all that, Gregory always found time for his one real passion, farming—in Okolona, he raised cotton, soybeans, hay, cattle, and quarter horses. "I always loved farming," he says.

At the end of his career, Gregory knew the Giants were rebuilding and knew there was little space for an outspoken veteran on the bench. "So I went in and told Mr. Mara that I had no future there and it probably would be better for everyone if I left," he says. He got his release and went back for one final season with Cleveland (a mistake he now regrets, he says, because he could have gone to powerhouses like Dallas and Oakland and played for winners) before going back home. There he built his own house, which, along with having his own farm, was the real fulfillment of his "lifelong dream."

After retiring, Gregory also added a few more activities to his résumé, including scouting part-time for the Denver Broncos for a few years and starting a business that buys, upholsters, and resells furniture. Today, he rents the land out to other farmers and no longer does the auctioneering as frequently as he once did, but it's not because he's slowing down—it's just that he's had a new role for the last twelve years: executive director of the Mississippi Association of Supervisors, an organization that acts as a liaison between the state legislature and elected officials. "There are eighty-two counties and 410 supervisors," he says, explaining that the association is a nonprofit group that lobbies at the state and occasionally federal levels. While he is personally a political conservative, he must maintain a balance in his job, although the state itself has become much more conservative in recent years.

Gregory may not be overtly political, but he has certainly become more politic in terms of speaking out. "I'm a little mellower and I've learned you have to know when to hold 'em and know when to fold 'em," he says. But being tactful doesn't mean that he's not the same old straight-ahead guy he was back when he was "Big Jack" anchoring the Giants defense. "I'm always going to be upfront with people. With me, what you see is what you get."

As a former punter, Dave Jennings knows how much even a short distance can matter. He has twice traveled far without every really going anywhere at all, and in the end he has come full circle.

That sounds confusing, but for Jennings it all makes sense—he was cut by the Giants after a lengthy career and finished out his playing days in the same stadium wearing the green of the Jets. Then he worked for years as the Jets' radio analyst before being unceremoniously dumped . . . only to be invited back into the embrace of the Giants family.

"Nothing surprises me anymore in the football or broadcasting businesses," says Jennings, who punted eleven seasons for the Giants and three for the Jets, then announced fourteen years for the Jets before returning to Big Blue in 2002.

Jennings, born in 1952, was raised in Garden City on Long Island, where he played high school basketball but not football. But as a freshman at St. Lawrence University, Jennings went with a friend to watch the freshman team practice. He was not impressed by the punters and told the coach he could do better—but because of basketball he would kick only in games and wouldn't have time to come to practice. The coach, Bob Sheldon, was wary until he saw Jennings cut loose, booting the ball 50 yards.

Although he played basketball all four years, he made a name for himself as a punter, and after graduating with a degree in economics, he was invited for a tryout by the Houston Oilers, who "had eleven punters and cut one a day." Two days after being released he got a call from the Giants, and soon began a lustrous career with the hometown team. (Growing up, however, Jennings had been a fan of the Los Angeles Rams, with their Fearsome Foursome defense.)

With the Giants, Jennings was named all-pro five times and led the league in 1980 with a 44.8-yard gross average. He was capable of kicking long or emphasizing hang time or direction or placing a kick out of bounds, whatever was needed. By the time he retired, he had set records for the most punts with 1,154 (later broken by longtime Giant Sean Landeta) and the most consecutive punts without a block, 623 from 1976 to 1983 (later broken by Chris Gardocki), thanks in part to his ability to keep his kicking leg hanging out front seemingly forever to ward off rushers.

But ask Jennings for a highlight among all those punts and all those years and it comes quickly: December 20, 1981, when the Giants had a chance to return to the playoffs for the first time since 1963.

"We had to beat Dallas, then hope the Jets beat the Packers," Jennings recalled. The game went into overtime and Dallas, hoping to take advantage of the thirty-mile-an-hour winds, chose to kick off and defend the east end goal. Sure enough, the Giants soon found themselves in dire straits, with a fourth down on their own five, the Cowboys' punt returner eagerly waiting, camped out on the Giants' 35-yard line.

But Jennings came through. "I had learned over the years the worst thing to do was to try to compensate for what the wind might do," he says. So Jennings let loose, nailing a 47-yard punt, which, combined with a 10-yard penalty, shoved the Cowboys well out of field goal range.

Discouraged, the Cowboys fumbled, Lawrence Taylor recovered, and the Giants mustered a field goal, eking out a 13–10 win that led them to the playoffs the next day and helped the team begin gaining momentum. "If I had made a poor punt, we wouldn't have made the playoffs," says Jennings. "That was the most exciting thing."

Jennings points out that the NFL record book game capsule highlights his kick. And Jennings, who still relishes watching the game tape with announcer John Madden declaring, "This place is rocking," after Jennings's punt, says Bill Parcells once told him it was the best punt he had ever seen.

After eleven years with the Giants, however, Jennings was cut after 1984 following a poor year. The Jets, knowing that Jennings handled Giants Stadium better than anyone, immediately snapped him up. "That was strange," he says, adding that the Jets were very good to him, even giving him his number, 13, even though Don Maynard had worn it.

After three more solid seasons in a foreign uniform in his home stadium, Jennings was released by the Jets. But he was hired almost immediately to become the analyst for their radio broadcasts. "It was exactly what I wanted to do," Jennings says.

The Jets didn't hire an unproven ex-jock simply because he was a familiar face. "I started doing broadcasting my second year in the league because I didn't know how long my punting career would last and I realized I should begin thinking right away about what I'd do when I was done," he says.

So Jennings sought pointers from and paid special attention to announcers Marty Glickman and Marv Albert. Then in 1976, he began doing high school basketball play-by-play for WNHC-AM in New Haven, Connecticut. When his career finally did wind down and Jennings landed the radio gig and then a second role on television with the MSG Network, he was ready.

Jennings enjoyed his years in the Jets organization—"they were terrific to me"—and won strong praise for his incisive and honest analysis. "I was taught by Marty Glickman to announce in a way that the fans could talk about the game the next day as if they'd been there."

Jennings earned a reputation for his detailed knowledge of the game, especially the rules. He credits his Giants special teams coach, a guy by the name of Bill Belichick, who was "phenomenal in his knowledge and preparation" as inspiration and adds that the league makes it easy. "The NFL actually encourages you to call the officiating office with questions," he says.

Then, out of nowhere, in 2002 the Jets made a much-criticized decision and dumped Jennings. But Jennings wasn't left out in the cold very long. The ex-punter, still a gym rat, went to work out near his Upper Saddle River, New Jersey, home. When he returned there were already two phone calls from the Giants, saying they had already contacted WFAN and wanted Jennings to come back home.

"I was as touched by that response as I have ever been in my life," Jennings says. "Mr. Mara always talks about 'Once you're a Giant, you're always a Giant.' And it was a thrill to come back home."

But before he could say yes, Jennings had one call to make. He rang up Dick Lynch, the Giants' reigning radio analyst, and asked if he'd be willing to share the booth with a third voice. (Bob Papa handles play-by-play.) "I would not have taken the job if Dick had a problem with it," he says, adding that in the end the men proved able to work comfortably together.

Jennings remains passionate about the game and his gig, saying, "Football is a year-round thing. I read books and fill notebooks to keep up to date." For instance, during a recent off-season he decided to research history's greatest defenses. In his digging, he uncovered gems like the time when the 1970s' Steel Curtain allowed only twenty-eight points over nine games.

It doesn't take much research for Jennings to come up with his most memorable moment so far in the Giants' booth. It came at the start of his very first game, the Hall of Fame game in Canton, Ohio. Just before the game began, Wellington Mara came into the booth without Jennings, who was looking out at the field. "He came over, put one arm around me, and whispered in my ear, 'Welcome home,'" Jennings recalls.

Bill Ellenbogen is not a household name in the world of Big Blue. Although he was a starter in the first-ever game at Giants Stadium, he's not someone who had a tremendous impact on Giants history: in his football career—as in his childhood and college career—it seemed the offensive lineman was just passing through on his way to somewhere else. It was only once his playing days ended that Ellenbogen settled down, but since then he has truly made his mark in a way that few ex-football players really do, becoming a household name and a force to be reckoned with in his adopted hometown of Blacksburg, Virginia.

Ellenbogen took a somewhat tortuous path to the Giants. His father owned a plastics factory in Rockland County, but his family gradually circled New York City—he was born in Glen Cove, then lived in Great Neck before his family moved to Spring Valley in Rockland County when he was seven and finally to New Rochelle when he was fifteen.

Ellenbogen's older brother, James, was not at all athletic and was highly intellectual—he is now a theoretical chemist dealing with nanotechnology and physics.

"I was built with more generous proportions and I took a different track into sports in part because of sibling rivalry, to establish my own niche," he says. Ellenbogen, who has a master's degree of his own, jokes that he's "the dummy in his family"—his younger brother, Richard, went on to get a master's degree in electrical engineering from Cornell.

Still, school always came first, even for the middle child. "My parents were very much into academics," says Ellenbogen, who as a boy first fancied himself a baseball player. "Sports was just something you do in your spare time—in eighth grade they wouldn't even sign the permission slip for me to play football." (His father would rarely come see him play in high school, college, or even the pros.)

In high school the following year Ellenbogen was allowed to play by his parents but only got in for two minutes of action in the season's last game. In the tenth and eleventh grades, Ellenbogen—who was small for his grade because he had skipped a year in school—was cut, and after moving to New Rochelle for his senior year, he managed to start in two games. He was not the kind of guy who had colleges looking for him—but his academic skill shone through and he earned a Regents Scholarship to the University of Buffalo.

But from his senior year of high school to his freshman year of college, Ellenbogen grew from 6'2" and 180 pounds to 6'4" and 210 pounds, so he was able to make the freshman team as a walk-on, starting at defensive end. He was red-shirted the following season and then given a partial scholarship in his junior year, during which he started for the varsity. But this was the late 1960s and the Buffalo campus was a hotbed of campus activism and not one with great interest in football. "No one came to the games," he says. "Then one day I was in my dorm room and I heard on the radio that Buffalo was dropping its football program. The coaches didn't even tell us."

Ellenbogen remembered how taken he had been with the "gorgeous surroundings" when the team had gone down to play Virginia Tech in Blacksburg, so he transferred there and, having filled out to 6'5" and 240 pounds, played two solid years as a defensive tackle. Still it was not surprising that he didn't get drafted, but Ellenbogen did not give up, instead calling around for a free-agent tryout.

"Football was my passion," he says. "It was so consuming it was an overriding obsession."

Ellenbogen wangled a shot with the Kansas City Chiefs. He was given an intelligence test and—in part because he was smart enough to remember varying snap counts—switched to the offensive line. While he forever regretted not having the chance to play defense, Ellenbogen never had the clout to push for what he wanted, and he says playing the line did gave him an edge over other free agents because he tended to make few mental mistakes.

He made it down to the last cut; when coach Hank Stram gave him the bad news he said he'd arrange for him to play for a friend who ran a semi-pro team back in Albany. And so Ellenbogen's "have desire, will travel" career was born. He spent that season with the Albany MetroMallers, getting paid $25 a game and earning another $9.35 an hour carrying pipe as an electrician in a job arranged by the team, helping to build the MetroMall project. "We'd practice a couple of nights a week, then play on Saturday," he recalls, adding that the quality of play was fairly good with six future pros on the team. "I was getting paid to play football. I thought I'd died and gone to heaven."

In the off-season Ellenbogen bulked up, adding twenty pounds of muscle. The Houston Oilers offered him an invitation to training camp and a $2,500 bonus. Unfortunately, 1974 was the year of labor strife and with the regular players picketing, free agents like Ellenbogen who were outside the union were given no choice by the teams—play or be gone. He went through six weeks of two-a-day drills in Huntsville, Texas, "where the climate felt like hell—it was 100 degrees and 97 percent humidity every day," he says, adding, "I'd lose fifteen pounds in water weight every practice and then gain it back."

When the veterans finally returned, the Oilers went through another four weeks of practice, but the established players were less than welcoming to their new teammates, whom they saw only as scabs. In the first day, Ellenbogen lined up opposite future Hall of Famer Elvin Bethea, whose uniform number he had been assigned during the labor situation. "He said, 'Listen, you motherfucker, you think you can cross the picket lines and wear my number,'" Ellenbogen recalls. And then, because Bethea was a superstar who didn't have to worry about making the team, "all he wanted to do was abuse me, so he hauled off and gave me a roundhouse."

Ellenbogen knew his status with the team was iffy at best, and when he saw the World Football League giving opportunities to players he knew he was equal to, he went to the Oilers and asked for his release. Sid Gillman initially said no, telling Ellenbogen he might make the team as a backup; Ellenbogen persisted, got his release, and went to the WFL's Philadelphia Bells, where he got to play regularly. (He says Gillman later got in trouble for stashing fifteen players on the taxi squad, which likely would have been Ellenbogen's fate.)

Then it was back to Blacksburg for the off-season, where Ellenbogen pursued his master's in education. "It was a great place to be young and single—there were college girls and great athletic facilities that I could use for free during the off-season," he says.

Ellenbogen, who went to the Washington Redskins camp that next season, says as a perpetual free agent he always had to arrive in camp in tip-top shape. "You are in such a tenuous position showing up each year with a different team," he says, explaining that the NFL is not played on a level playing field. "If you're undrafted or a free agent you don't get an equal look—the teams have invested heavily in those other players."

Additionally, veterans can "take a knee" during drills to protect their bodies, while the unproven must go all out on every play, suffering more wear and tear along the way. To counter that political disadvantage, Ellenbogen says, free agents need to do something to make a quick and memorable first impression. Since he couldn't catch a touchdown pass or sack a quarterback, Ellenbogen learned "to be really aggressive," even to the point of virtually starting fights. "You have to get the coach's attention, then hopefully you'll last till the exhibition games and then you can play well."

Ellenbogen made it to the last cut with the Redskins, but coach George Allen tended to favor veterans and, in the end, Ellenbogen was gone; he quickly found a gig in the newly reconstituted WFL, playing for $500 a game for a team in Shreveport, Louisiana.

Then, in 1976 Ellenbogen finally came to the Giants. Once again he made it to the last cut in training camp but failed to make the squad. "If I was getting cut very early in these training camps I might have gotten discouraged, but I made it to the last cut so I was always able to rationalize," he says, adding that in this case coach Bill Arnsparger thought he'd had a pretty good training camp.

"And I was still learning to play offense, which I was doing each year in training camp and trying to learn on the run. I was getting bigger and felt I was getting better. Ultimately, though, I just loved sports."

So he went off to the Canadian Football League on a ten-day trial contract with the Winnipeg Blue Bombers. But before the ten days were even up, the Giants had come calling again—offensive lineman Al Simpson got hurt in the second game and the team needed Ellenbogen and would even give him a chance to start.

"I was incredibly elated," Ellenbogen recalls. "I was going to play in the NFL. It was my life's dream. And this was validation—they had cut me and now they had to call me back to play."

In his first play, a toss-pitch that required everybody moving outside to block for running back Doug Kotar, Ellenbogen's task was to stop legendary defender Jack Youngblood by diving into the back of his legs. Youngblood ended up with a sprained ankle and stopped to curse out the rookie before leaving the field. "But it wasn't a dirty play and the coaches thought it was great. I was so jacked up on adrenaline that if they had said go run through a wall, I would have done it."

The next week the Giants came home for their first-ever game in Giants Stadium and Ellenbogen was named a starter. The stands were packed, the game was on national television, and the Cowboys were a premier team and a divisional rival. "Running out through that tunnel was an incredible rush," Ellenbogen remembers. "Still to this moment it was one of my life's high points."

Ellenbogen remained as a starter, and then when Simpson returned and John McVay took over as head coach, Ellenbogen and Simpson split time. But the following season, Ellenbogen was largely relegated to backup. "I was very frustrated," he says. "I had worked really hard and I had to watch us lose with the players ahead of me. I went to the coach and said, 'Why don't you give me a chance? If I do crappy, you can cut me. What do you have to lose?'"

Ellenbogen is realistic and says he doesn't know how he would have fared—"I might have stunk up the place"—but he couldn't have hurt the team any worse than the starters. But McVay wouldn't make any changes, and Ellenbogen suspects that the front office was pressuring him to keep highly paid and highly touted starters like John Hicks starting no matter what the results. "Good teams evaluate their investments on an ongoing basis; otherwise you just compound the original error," he says. "The Giants were more concerned about their image."

After the season Ellenbogen, who had largely been relegated to special teams, told a *Daily News* reporter about what had transpired and how he felt, and the paper slapped his name across the back-page headline: "Ellenbogen Angry." When Ellenbogen came back to the area in February for surgery on his dislocated shoulder, McVay let him know that he was "really disappointed" and felt betrayed by this act of disloyalty. "He said that my chance of making the team was not very good."

The team put Ellenbogen on waivers but when others expressed interest pulled him back and wouldn't trade him. Ellenbogen says he had an excellent training camp but that McVay was looking for an excuse to let him go and when he allowed San Diego's defensive tackle Gary "Big Hands" Johnson to get a sack off of him near the end of the preseason, Ellenbogen soon found himself out of a job. McVay, of course, had held onto him so long that now NFL teams had their roster spots filled.

Looking back, Ellenbogen says that his strong personality and outspoken approach probably hurt his football career, adding that he may have gone too far in giving those quotes to the *Daily News*. "I've learned the hard way to choose my words more carefully and that a word, once spoken, can never be reclaimed," he says.

McVay did tell Ellenbogen of a roster spot with Toronto back in the CFL, and he jumped at the chance because the pay was so good. "I sold out and I regret that," Ellenbogen says. "If I had gone back to Blacksburg and waited a couple of weeks another NFL team may have had an injury and I would have gotten a call."

Compounding matters, Ellenbogen was the one who ended up injured, his season finished by knee surgery. He was back in Toronto in 1979 but was "really dispirited—I was twenty-eight and my career was on the wane." He got cut and latched on with Montreal and then Winnipeg, where he suffered a bad ankle injury. (He has since had surgery on his knee and his back from another football injury and expects to need more.) That was the end, he thought—no more training camps. But in 1980 he had healed and gave the NFL one more try, with the Atlanta Falcons. Again, he made it to the last cut, but he was no up-and-coming youngster anymore and when he was let go he realized his career was over.

After growing up in three counties, attending two different colleges, going to eight training camps, and playing on eleven teams in four different leagues, Ellenbogen was ready to end his "peripatetic" ways and settle down, and he knew Blacksburg would be his home. Still, Ellenbogen confesses, "I didn't know what I wanted to be when I grew up. Football was my passion and when I quit I was kind of lost."

Every time Ellenbogen had been cut, his dad would call and ask him to come home and work in the factory, which he really did not want to do. He didn't want to coach because it would require moving around again. He contemplated a PhD in the physiology of exercise and along the way he had bought a couple of rental properties as an investment and gotten his real estate license, but the PhD seemed like too much and with interest rates at 18 percent the real estate market was dead. Having never earned more than $37,000 a year, Ellenbogen couldn't sit around waiting for inspiration, so he began bartending locally in Blacksburg.

Then in 1982, he opened a restaurant inside an old home, calling it Bogen's. (The following year he opened another in nearby Radford called BT's, but he sold that after a year; Bogen's he owned until 2004.) Gradually, he found two other things he felt as deeply and strongly about as football, and since then Ellenbogen has devoted himself to both: his family (his wife, Janet, and teenage children, Matt and Courtney) and Blacksburg itself. "I developed a passion for Blacksburg," he says, adding with a sense of wonder that if not for Buffalo canceling its football program, he might never have found this place.

"I've made a commitment to it. I feel a great sense of moral obligation to treat the community as well as it has treated me."

And so he began a second life as a developer pushing for "smart development" and as a community leader. "Walkable and livable communities have become buzzwords, but I've been working on it a long time," Ellenbogen says. "It's an ethos—it's something I espouse at seminars."

Although Blacksburg is a town of just forty thousand, dominated by Virginia Tech, it is gradually urbanizing, "like a slow train wreck," so Ellenbogen has pushed to preserve trails and open space. He points to the lessons of history and visionary planning like the development of Central Park on what is now the world's most valuable real estate. "Once you build up an area, you can't go back."

Among his projects have been a low-impact development called Coal Bank Ridge, which was initially controversial but which features only fifty-two homes spread out among 225 acres; most roofs are kept below treetops and nearly half the acreage was placed in a conservation easement. Locally, he's also known as one of the forces behind the Huckleberry Trail, a six-mile paved bikeway and footpath that he steered to completion over nine years, and for Gateway Park, which connects the town to the adjoining national forest. "Blacksburg is right on the edge of this forest, but there was no access—it was all private property," Ellenbogen explains, so he and another local resident bought property for the town to create Gateway Park, which they now hope to link to the Huckleberry Trail. "That adds 100,000 acres to the town, in a way. That's something you can put on a brochure."

Ellenbogen still often finds himself caught in the middle of those who want no development at all and those who exploit the lack of coordinated planning and regulation to create bad developments. "You can't stop change, but the key is to direct it and make your area change intelligently," he says, adding that he now believes a town can't plan smart growth without a regional plan or all that happens is that the sprawl begins right outside the town limits. "You have to do countywide planning at least—there are five Wal-Marts within twenty miles of here. That's not planning."

Ellenbogen says coming of age in the 1960s helped him develop a sense of social and moral obligation as well as "a more reasoned approach to profit making. I want to make a profit, but the bottom line is not the only thing we should look at," he says. "I believe you can do real estate and can make money and do good things at the same time."

G ary Shirk is ready to prove himself. Always has been, always will be. These days, he's always putting himself on the line in his fast-moving, ever-changing transportation job, overseeing the movement of shipping containers on trains. But for much of his life he was hard at work proving to everyone who said he was too small, or too slow, or too whatever that they were wrong, that he belonged.

"My whole career I always thought everyone was better and that I had to prove I belonged," Shirk says. "I never went to training camp thinking I had the team made—that's just not my nature. I always felt I had to prove myself, and I think that's one of my best attributes."

So prove himself he did, at Morehead State, where he was named captain; in the World Football League, where he earned a starting job in the pros; with the Giants, where at one point he caught ninety-four passes in a three-year span as the Giants' starting tight end; and finally in the United States Football League, where he showed he still had some football left in him.

Shirk grew up on a farm eight miles outside of Marysville, Ohio, which itself is thirty miles northwest of Columbus. "We would work hard every day there," he says, adding that his background ensured that he remained grounded even as he began achieving athletic success. "If my head wasn't on straight, my dad would make sure it would get back on straight."

Working with the animals and baling hay appealed to Shirk, who says that during high school he focused on farming more than on the idea that he might one day attend college—at one point he was helping raise twelve Angus cows and helping oversee four hundred acres of land. "This was not gardening," he says. "This was farming. We worked at it."

As a result, Shirk was always strong, farmboy strong. "I never lifted weights, but I was stronger than most of the others from farming and I always had durability in the heat," he says. Shirk performed better on defense than offense in high school. "I really

shined on defense, but our offense went backwards most of the time, kind of like the Giants teams I played on," he says, adding that he contributed more offensively in basketball, where he was all-conference and the leading scorer.

The 178-pounder had no scholarship offers, but his coach convinced him to go down to Kentucky, where he was ready to prove himself as a walk-on for defensive end at Morehead State University, where he faced a typical "no promises" offer.

"They said, 'You're too late for a scholarship now, but if you earn one you'll get one,'" he says. "Even after they saw me they said, 'You may not play, and if you do it will be as a tight end.'" (The team had a graduating senior at tight end but four defensive ends coming back.)

But, he says, it was the story of his life. "In my whole career I always was told, 'We won't make you any promises, but if you show you're good enough you'll get a shot.'"

No promises? No matter. He earned a full scholarship, caught ninety passes in his years at Morehead and eventually made all-conference for three straight years, demonstrated his toughness by playing with two broken arms at one point, and became the team's captain. "It was just a fantastic career, but it was not the kind of career that got you drafted," he says, "but I was saying, 'Maybe I'll get a shot.'"

Still, when he did attract scouts in his senior year most of what he heard was negative: "They'd say, 'You're only 6'1",' or 'You only run a 4.8 40 and we're looking for guys who can run a 4.6.'"

But the New York Jets came down and told him they'd draft him, albeit in the sixteenth or seventeenth round. "I didn't care when I went, as long as I was drafted," he says. "But draft day came and draft day went and there was no phone call, not a word."

It turned out the Jets still were interested in Shirk but knew no one else would draft him so they used their picks on others, planning to invite him to their free-agent camp later on. In the meantime, Shirk planned on a job back home in Ohio as a teacher and assistant coach at a local high school. Then he got the call from the Jets offering a plane ticket and a car to pick him up and take him to their tryouts at Hofstra University. He was flattered, optimistic, and impressed . . . until he got there.

"When the car picks you up at the airport you say, 'Well, okay, this is a big deal,' but then you get there and it looks like they're giving something away for free—there are just guys everywhere," he says.

It turned out that the Jets had invited 304 players to camp; even worse, they'd neglected to tell Shirk that they weren't planning on giving him a shot at tight end. "The coach said, 'We're sorry about the draft but we're glad to see you. Oh, and by the way, today we're going to try you at linebacker,'" Shirk recalls.

Shirk tried explaining that as a tight end he'd spent the last four years running forward, not backward or sideways as a linebacker does, but to no avail. His 4.8 40 was actually the fastest of the twenty-nine linebacker hopefuls'—"they were a pretty pathetic group"—but when he had to cover running backs coming out of the backfield, the gig was up. "I just grabbed hold of the guy, because I sure wasn't going to keep up with him," he says.

Shirk was disappointed afterward, but he realizes that in the end things worked out for the best—had he made the team he would have been buried on the bench or maybe on special teams and might never have had the chance to play regularly, but by being forced to go to the WFL he showed the NFL that he at least deserved a shot at tight end.

At the time, however, Shirk thought playing football was a thing of the past, so he settled in as a teacher, also putting in time as offensive coordinator for the football team and with the freshman basketball and track teams as well. "I was married and teaching out in a little school in the country, and we were fine," he says.

Then one Sunday morning Shirk was grading midterms when his wife asked if he'd be coming to church—much to her dismay he said that he had to get his papers marked. But while she was gone the phone rang. It was the Toronto Northmen of the fledgling World Football League offering him more than three times his schoolteacher salary to come play football.

"When my wife came home I said, 'Guess who called,' and she was still annoyed and she said, 'I really don't want to hear about it,'" he says with a laugh, adding that he told her about the call anyway but left the part about the huge pay raise till the very end.

Before Shirk got to Toronto, however, the team moved to Memphis (where they were awkwardly renamed the Southmen, although they did show some prescience by wearing grizzlies on their helmets). And when he got to Memphis, it was the same old story. The rosters were small—only thirty-seven guys—and there was a tight end in front of him with a guaranteed contract. No promises from the team? No matter. Shirk outplayed everyone, and, under coach John McVay, he started for two years there, catching forty-nine passes. By playing alongside guys like John Huarte, Larry Csonka, Paul Warfield, and Jim Kiick he demonstrated his professionalism, and when the league folded Shirk attracted interest from the Los Angeles Rams, the Washington Redskins, and the Giants.

"The WFL definitely helped me develop how I play," he says, adding that later, when the Giants would bring in rookies to try to displace him, they never really had a chance to learn the game and create their own style the way he had.

He was awed by the plush training facilities at Redskins Park and by the sheer presence of head coach George Allen. "I would have signed in a second," he says, except that when Allen opened his mouth, the first thing to come out was, "You're awful short to be a tight end." Right away Shirk knew the team would never give him a fair shot, would never let him show that he could indeed block out L. C. Greenwood or "Too Tall" Jones.

When he got to New York, Shirk was not so impressed with the Giants facilities at Pace University, but he received a cordial welcome from Giants great Andy Robustelli, then director of operations, and was told by coach Bill Arnsparger that he'd get a fair shake because McVay had recommended him. Shirk was sold on New York, even though the coach also warned him that he already had the well-respected Bob Tucker as the starter and a highly talented young tight named Jim Obradovich as a backup and he would only keep two tight ends.

No promises? No matter. Arnsparger said, "If you're good enough, you'll make the club," and that was all Shirk needed to hear. Obradovich ended up the odd man out, spending his career in San Francisco and Tampa Bay. In his rookie year Shirk was indeed stuck behind Tucker but learned a lot from the veteran.

"He was the slowest tight end in the world—he made me feel like a defensive back—but he was smart and he ran these routes and had these head fakes and cuts and no one could cover him,"

Shirk says. "It was amazing. You just had to learn from watching him."

Still, it was difficult adjusting to life in New York for the small-town Shirk, especially since the Giants were still playing home games on the road as they awaited their new stadium and since they went 0-9 in his introduction to NFL life.

But after McVay took over as head coach and then traded Tucker the next year, Shirk emerged as a force in the offense—or as much of a force as you could be in the Giants offense of the 1970s. (In addition, he was always a crucial member of special teams—with the brutal job of being "wedge captain.") In his second season, he caught sixteen passes, averaging 17.5 yards per catch. He truly emerged in 1979, the rookie year for another Morehead State graduate, a passer by the name of Phil Simms. That year Shirk led the team with thirty-one catches, contributing 471 yards. Then in the 1981 season he pulled in forty-two passes for 445 yards, including one game where he grabbed eleven.

But one thing Shirk never led the Giants in was job security—every year the coaching staff looked at the slow, undersized tight end and decided that someone else could do the job better. Then they'd bring in a newcomer—Al Dixon, Cleveland Jackson, Loaird McCreary, Boyd Brown, Tom Mullady, Dave Young, or Robert Hubble—and soon find out that Shirk was better than them all.

Shirk was often motivated by their slights, although that doesn't mean he liked it—he always said athletes play better when someone believes in them, although coaches rarely showed that faith in him up front.

"Ray Perkins believed in motivation by threat," he says. "In 1979 I led the team in receptions and the next year I still came to mini-camp ready to play—I was always ready to play. But after mini-camp he comes up to me and says, 'I'm going to get someone to take your spot.' For me that just fueled the fire."

Bill Parcells showed a similar lack of confidence in Shirk—he kept him on the Giants roster after taking over in 1983, which prevented Shirk from going to play for the New Jersey Generals, but then cut him before the NFL season began. (Despite his problems with the coaches, Shirk loved the Giants organization. "There was no better person than Wellington Mara. Look at what happened with Doug Kotar [who died of cancer]. If you got hurt, they'd take care of you—on other teams they'd drag you off and lay you on the side and if you're still there tomorrow they'd dig a hole for you.")

Shirk's days with the Giants were finally over, but he didn't want his football days to end till he thought they should. Although he would have loved to play for New Jersey, which would have meant more time at home with his family, in 1984 he landed a job back in Memphis—a two-year guaranteed contract, the first guarantee he'd ever had.

"Missing a season at that point in your career and life is the hardest thing in the world," Shirk says. But, of course, he had something to prove, so he whipped himself into shape and promptly went out and caught fifty-seven passes. "That was the greatest thing in the world for me."

After his second year the USFL was done, but that was okay because Shirk was done too. "I was ready to quit because my body told me it was time," he says. Shirk was able to spend more time with his two daughters and particularly with his son, Jeff, who took all his father's lessons about hustle and hard work to heart. He played both lacrosse and football in high school in New Jersey. "I wish I had his hands and touch—he could catch anything," Shirk says. Unfortunately, he adds, "He also had his dad's speed and that kind of hurt him. But he was very good at lacrosse so I pushed him a little more toward lacrosse."

Jeff Shirk won a scholarship to the University of Maryland and went on to star on the Terrapins' national championship lacrosse team with his father always in attendance, at home and on the road. He then went on a four-year pro career and is now an assistant lacrosse coach back at Maryland.

His dad would have loved coaching, but he didn't like the lack of job security. "The trouble with coaching is that coaches always get fired," he says.

So after his playing days Shirk moved into the transportation field. Actually, he'd already had a foot in it since 1979, when he and his friend John Hicks had bought three semis. "He lost interest pretty quickly and said, 'You do the work,' which was fine with me because I'm kind of a control freak," Shirk says.

But for the last fifteen years, Shirk has worked for Maerst, a steamship company; he oversees domestic double-stacks, putting containers onto trucks and trains. "In my office I have trucks and trains on my windowsill—it's like being a little kid," he says, adding that in 2001 he moved from the company's Morristown, New Jersey, office to its office in Charlotte, North Carolina.

Besides the job security, Shirk also loves the fact that he has to prove himself every day in a constantly changing world. "Things change every second in this business—if something goes wrong with the railroad or with a trucker, your customer is going to be yelling at you, you have to prove yourself today," he says.

"I ran special teams the whole time I was in the pros because I was good at it and because that's what was needed. This job is a lot like special teams. Every day is different and you always have to adapt. You have to rise to the occasion."

J im Clack knows about adversity and about comebacks, in sports and in life. He knows from the time he scored the winning basket for the state basketball championship only to have his father die weeks later; he knows from the time he returned from retirement to help lead the Giants to their first playoff game in eighteen years; he knows from the time he was in a car crushed by an eighteen-wheeler and had to rebuild his entire life afterward; and he knows from his current battle with cancer, which he has survived and even used to motivate and inspire others.

Clack's entire story—and he's a wonderful storyteller, with a knack for dramatic details—is inspirational, so much so that he has recently been included in one of those *Chicken Soup for the Soul* books. But it is inspiring in large part because it hasn't been easy—his accomplishments have been marked by his ability to endure the most difficult of situations.

To make it as a football player, Clack first had to overcome the toughest kind of challenge: the disapproval of his father. He grew up in Rocky Mount, North Carolina, with a hero to worship right nearby: "My father was my mentor and the greatest guy in the world," he says. His father, Linwood, ran a local grocery store, and after practice and on weekends it went without saying that Jim would be in there helping out and cleaning up. "He taught me a great work ethic."

Linwood didn't like football much—he'd go out in the backyard to play Wiffle ball or basketball with young Jim (in basketball, Jim would always choose to be North Carolina while Dad would pick Wake Forest—the school Jim would someday attend). And so in Jim's freshman year of high school he played basketball, and during the football games he was playing bass drum in the band. "Finally, the coach said, 'Jim, you're too big to carry that drum—why don't you come play football,'" Clack recalls, adding that the coach persuaded his father to say yes.

And so Clack found himself playing defensive end, but on the first series of downs, after getting clipped from behind, he found himself lying on the ground with a broken ankle. "All of a sudden I see a Fiesta Oldsmobile station wagon driving across the field before the emergency crews could make a move," he recalls. His father loaded him into the family wagon and took him to the hospital. "He wasn't too happy about it because I couldn't play basketball that year."

Yet Linwood let Jim go out for football the following year and Jim gave him plenty to cheer about, on the field and on the court. Playing linebacker for the varsity as a sophomore, he grabbed a tipped pass at his own 6-yard line and ran 94 yards on a dead run for a touchdown, prompting this postgame analysis from his dad: "You know what, son, I think I'm going to like this game." Then came the state championship game in Greensboro for the school basketball team. The game went into double overtime, and at the end there was a missed shot bouncing away from the basket when Clack appeared to tap home the winning shot.

When Clack came home the next day, his father was sitting on the porch clipping articles about the game out of the newspaper. The reason, he explained, "was that I want you to know how proud I am of you if I'm not there to tell you," Clack recalls. It may have seemed an odd statement at the time, but Clack's father knew something he hadn't told Jim and his two sisters: he had known for months that he had a heart condition that left him vulnerable to fatal heart attacks. A week later he died of a heart attack at his store.

Clack struggled to stay on track but found other father figures who helped straighten him out. For college, he almost did choose North Carolina—he had played basketball each summer for Dean Smith and the legendary hoops coach wanted Clack as a sixth man, but Clack knew, given his build, that football would be his primary sport, and he didn't like UNC's football coach. So he chose Wake Forest instead. There he studied political science and history, planning to become an attorney eventually. "I love to argue and arbitrate and play devil's advocate. I always want to take the other side," he says.

But it seemed that the small lineman did not impress coach Bill Tate. "He told me I'd be the third-team left tackle," Clack says. So Clack left school and went home to work in a store till school started up again in the fall. But the trainer and some players persuaded Clack to come back. "I told Coach Tate I wanted a chance to earn the position back," he recalls, "and I pancaked the guy opposite me three times in a row and then said, 'Coach, give me that black jersey.'" (The black jersey was for starters.)

Clack then became a starter, but his relationship with Tate remained strained. Then his senior year, although he weighed just 217 pounds, he managed to catch the attention of the pros. "I was playing tackle and I had a really good game against North Carolina going up against Mike Smith, who was pretty much all-world," he says. Soon after, Art Rooney of the Pittsburgh Steelers asked someone at UNC who "that little guy was who beat up Mike Smith," and when he found who it was, he asked how far it was to Wake Forest, jumped in his car, and drove off. At Wake Forest, Clack says, Rooney walked around asking, "Where can I find Jimmy Clack?" ("Back then I was Jimmy, but when you get to the NFL you have to be tough, so everybody called me Jim," Clack says.) Rooney told the youngster that Pittsburgh was interested in drafting him. Clack, who knew by then that he had what it took athletically to play in the NFL, was elated.

But draft day came and went with no call. The next day too. Finally, on the third day, coach Chuck Noll called up and said the team hadn't drafted him but would sign Clack as a free agent, with a bonus of $500. "I thought I was wealthy," he says. But a new obstacle was in his way. The rookie coach ultimately decided not to take a chance on an undersized lineman and cut Clack. Noll did it again in 1970.

Still, Clack refused to give up. After the first time, he went and played for the semi-pro minor league Norfolk Neptunes, working to bulk up his frame. It was not fun—he was being paid by the Steelers and so didn't have to work during the day as his teammates did, and he didn't play regularly since he was mostly there to build his physique. "I was an outcast," he says. The following year he stayed in Pittsburgh on the taxi squad. Finally he made the team in 1971; by 1973, as the Steelers emerged as the dominant team in the NFL, Clack was emerging as a valuable regular on the offensive line, spending time at both guard and tackle.

After having what he thought was his best season ever in 1977, Clack had his agent ask for more money. (This was especially necessary because Clack was going through a divorce from a wife who had just built a mansion with his money.) "I was never a confrontational guy but I thought I deserved it," he says, adding that he went home to Rocky Mount expecting to perhaps hold out at the start of training camp. Instead, he was traded to the Giants, who gave up only failed lineman John Hicks, who never even played a down in Pittsburgh. "The worst part wasn't leaving the Steelers because we were winning and the Giants weren't but because the players there were as great as people as they were as players," he says.

Additionally, Pittsburgh was a conservative town and a good fit for a small-town kid, and some folks commented about "little Jimmy Clack going off to New York City." Yet Clack fell in love with the city itself, checking out pretty much everything on Broadway and as many restaurants as he could. And at first, he felt really comfortable with the Giants, who were run, like the Steelers, by an old NFL family. "My first day there Mr. Mara came down and we talked more about Mr. Rooney than about anything else," he recalls. And the Giants wanted him exclusively at center, no more bouncing to guard and back as he had in Pittsburgh.

The 1978 season started off in promising enough fashion, but then came The Fumble. What was worse than the play itself from Clack's point of view was its aftermath: "We went back into the locker room and everybody just started arguing with each other," he says, adding that this sort of sniping and finger-pointing would never have happened in Pittsburgh and was directly related to the team's subsequent collapse that season. "I went to the phone and called my agent saying I wanted to be traded."

But Clack stuck it out, becoming the team captain and a three-time Pro Bowler with the Giants before finally deciding that he could no longer give 100 percent of himself physically. After starting forty-eight straight games at center for the team, his knees were shot. So before the 1981 season—just months after signing a new two-year deal worth more than $100,000 a year—he went and told coach Ray Perkins he was through. He worked out an agreement on the deal with the Giants and then had arthroscopic surgery to remove bone chips from both knees. Then he returned to Rocky Mount, where he restored Victorian homes and owned a sporting goods store, two hair salons, and other businesses to keep him busy. "I was really enjoying life," he says.

But with the chips out of his knees he was also feeling much better and was playing basketball regularly to keep in shape. So when new Giants starter Ernie Hughes went down with a knee injury in November, Clack suddenly got a call from Perkins asking if he could come back to the team. In fact, Perkins asked if he could come back that Sunday and start against Washington. Clack did—although he let a new rookie keep his old number, 56 (it was a guy by the name of Lawrence Taylor)—and helped lead a recharged offensive line to create holes for new running back Rob Carpenter. This was a real team effort, he says. "This time we came together."

Clack thought about coming back again in 1982 and feels he probably could have but decided that being part of that playoff season in 1981 was a "good way to go out." (As a players' rep for the union, he may not have enjoyed 1982 anyway, since the season was derailed by labor issues.)

Back in retirement, Clack plunged into a new business venture, one that would test just about anyone's resiliency: the restaurant business. He and a partner opened up three restaurants in North Carolina (including one in Rocky Mount) in Victorian buildings renovated by Clack. "It was the toughest business I was ever in," he says. "I loved the challenge, but it was just too many hours."

One night in 1985 at his hometown restaurant Clack had had too much to drink and eat and gave the keys to his wife to drive home. But she pulled out in front of an eighteen-wheeler that was going too fast on Route 301, and the next thing Clack knew he was pinned inside his car for two hours—actually, he didn't really know that, since among his injuries he suffered memory loss from ten days before the accident to seven days afterward. He was in intensive care and then laid up on his back for a long time.

The pain he suffered was only half the problem. "Absentee ownership in the restaurant business is not a good thing," he says with a wry chuckle, adding that right before the accident he had been notified by the IRS that he owed interest and penalties going back four years on a deal that his accountant had told him was a legitimate tax write-off. "When I got out I was flat broke and my career was off track."

It took him a while to find himself, but finally he did, in 1989, when Bill Brooks spoke to a group of ex-footballers about his sales and management training company called The Brooks Group. "He talked about how winning teams like the Steelers understood great management, and that got my attention," Clack recalls. He was disappointed to learn that there were no opportunities for him at that time, but two months later he got a call from Brooks asking if he was interested in making a training video for Isuzu Trucks. "I was nervous and didn't think I was all that great but I guess I was natural and they liked my intensity," Clack says.

Brooks liked Clack enough that by 1994 Clack was president of the company, handling clients ranging from Mack Trucks to Sara Lee and traveling 150 days a year to give speeches and help run seminars in sales training, service training, sales management, and leadership skills.

He loved it, but he admits, "I was pushing myself too hard." Unfortunately, it took another true test of his resiliency to slow him down. In 2002, Clack went to his doctor for a checkup and they discovered cancer on his tonsil. He went to an oncologist who removed it only to have a huge mass the size of a tennis ball bulge out on Clack's neck. "The tonsil was restricting the cancer," Clack says, adding that the doctors told him he'd been carrying it for some time—it was stage 4 cancer—and the prognosis was not good. Yet Clack defied the odds and survived by undergoing a brutal radiation treatment. "I was so beat up and worn out, I couldn't talk at all," he says. "Nothing is as traumatic as having this. I have been through a lot. My wife Susan and my dog Lizzie were all that got me through it."

Clack, who lost forty pounds during the treatment, still has scars on his lymph nodes—one doctor wants to remove the nodes, the other doesn't—and he lives with the everyday fear that the cancer could return at any point. He also knows he can't push himself as much as he had in the past. So in late 2003, he told Brooks what he had told Ray Perkins—that he could no longer give 100 percent and so he was leaving. But this time he was going out on his own—Brooks let him take some of his own clients and Clack is running his own training company now.

"I get to call my own shots and set my own schedule," he says, adding that as a start-up business he'll reach out for new clients through his self-named website. "I'm very excited about it. I love working with people and I still want to do this for another fifteen years if I'm still here."

But he's also realizing that there's something else he wants to do. "I want to help crusade against cancer." And since he loves working with people, he especially wants to reach out to others who have gone through what he has, to let them know he understands what they're feeling. "I'm trying to get involved speaking to cancer groups," he says, even though his voice has not fully recovered. "One lady came up to me after an event and told me about her cancer and I just said to her afterwards to call me any time she wants. Cancer is something we have to live with every day now."

Beasley Reece, sports director and anchor for Philadelphia's KWY (CBS-3), is not your typical ex-jock on television, the kind whose face is on the screen because of its celebrity, not the brain and skills behind it. The speedy Reece was a key component of the Giants' defense as the team inched from perpetual mediocrity back up to competitive respectability (although he was gone when the revival was completed in the 1986 Super Bowl season). But he took his first steps toward a successful broadcast career well before he ever put on a pro uniform.

Born and raised in Waco, Texas, Reece gave a speech in high school one day that caught the attention of a guidance counselor, who told the youngster he should think about a career in broadcasting.

"He took me down to the local radio station, KWTX, and got me a job there," Reece says. Reece did a little of everything, including "ripping script" to run it into the newsroom. But more significant than what he did was who he met—local radio star Dave South took Reece under his wing, teaching him about broadcasting and, most importantly, how to eliminate "my strong Texas twang."

Not that Reece was so quick to leave small-town Texas behind—he went to North Texas State University, where he studied music and—no surprise—journalism. After making the football team there as a walk-on, he became a star. He then had the greatest thrill imaginable when the Dallas Cowboys, who had just made it to the Super Bowl, drafted him. "That was absolutely the ultimate high," he says.

It didn't last long—"I wasn't mature enough and didn't know enough about football," he says, but also the Cowboys drafted a bunch of other cornerbacks and tried shifting Reece to wide receiver, where he struggled. Just before his second season, America's Team dumped him.

"I was the last player cut—we were in the stands taking the team photos when they pulled me out," he recalls of that day in 1977.

Reece was devastated but bounced back quickly when he found

a team with more openings than the Cowboys. "The Giants were so needy as an organization that they asked me whether I wanted to play wide receiver, running back, or cornerback," he says. Reece asked what the team needed most, but he was ready to return to defense anyway, since being a wide receiver "was my first experience in being unsuccessful."

This Giant welcome "immediately wiped the [Cowboy] star off my heart," Reece says. "It made me a Giants fan for life."

But while he was no longer a Cowboy, he was still a cowboy, even if the twang was gone. "I flew to New York and the equipment manager sees me get off in blue jeans, a cowboy shirt, and a big belt buckle with my initials on it, he looks me up and down and says, 'We're going to have to teach you how to dress up here.' "

Although Reece eventually grew to love New York, the initial culture shock was tremendous. "I felt like I'd moved to another country," he says. "Ernie Jones and I debated when we would be ready to go through the Lincoln Tunnel to New York—we were afraid we would not be able to find our way out. We were in north New Jersey for almost a month before we went in."

And that first trip didn't last long. This was the '70s, of course, when Times Square was at its sleaziest. "Everything had at least three Xs and some had five—those had to have animals in it—and our chins were to our chest." The two made a brief stop at Nathan's, where they were shocked and dismayed by the homeless guys scavenging for food—"it was a heartbreaker; I bought hot dogs for four guys"—then got out of there as quickly as they could.

Reece says it wasn't until his third season, when he had played tour guide to his parents a few times, that he really became comfortable in the city. That was also the year he really began establishing himself at safety, after two years battling serious leg injuries. He had 117 tackles, including 75 solo, and three fumble recoveries. He followed up in 1980 with three interceptions and twenty-four kick returns for 471 yards; the following year he had four interceptions for 84 yards and recovered one fumble for a touchdown.

Reece made enough of a name for himself that an actress named Allyce Tannenberg, about to take the role of Mrs. DiPesto in the television series *Moonlighting*, decided that she'd take her stage name from her boyfriend's favorite football player and remade herself as Allyce Beasley.

Although Reece's favorite on-field moment was a diving inter-ception against St. Louis, his most memorable experience with the Giants came in the locker room. In 1981, the Giants finally had become good again. "We'd been through a lot and I was slow to realize it," Reece says. "I didn't realize how good Lawrence Taylor was at first—he was the difference. Just after midseason I had an awakening."

Then in the season's last game, the Giants squeaked past Dallas, but they would make the playoffs only if the Jets beat Green Bay. The team gathered at the stadium, barbecuing and watching the game together. After the game Wellington Mara spoke to the group, the first time in Reece's career the owner addressed the whole team.

"He told us what it meant to him personally and to the organiza-tion, to feel pride and respect again," Reece says, getting choked up as he recalls the moment. "That was by far the greatest mo-ment—I'm fifty now and I still get emotional about it."

But in 1982, Reece, the players' union representative, devoted much of his time to the players' strike and was unprepared for the season when it finally arrived. After his poor season, the Giants made Terry Kinard their top draft choice, and when Kinard won the starting job midway through 1983, Reece, who already had two pick-offs, asked to be waived rather than sent to the bench. He was immediately snapped up by Tampa Bay, where he snapped up another six interceptions in the second half of the season. He played one more season for Tampa Bay.

By the time he retired, Reece was more than ready for his next career. He had cultivated contacts in the media in New York and even landed a sports show on cable television, then in its infancy, where he interviewed the man who invented Nautilus equipment and showed arthroscopic surgery on television. "I had tapes ready to hand people, so that was a big advantage," he says. "Within a week of retiring I had two stations in Florida offering me a job."

Reece began at tiny WTOG in St. Petersburg, a station where he had to do everything for himself from shooting to editing. ("These days if I touch any machine, I get arrested by the union," he jokes.) His break came three years later, when a general manager from a Connecticut station was on vacation in Florida and knew that Re-ece's Giants connection, combined with his developing skills, would be a perfect fit. So it was on to WVIT in Hartford, where Reece earned four local Associated Press awards for his work and eventually moved up to sports director. He also made a name for himself in a more unusual way.

WVIT's competitor had hired a new sports anchor whose signature work was *Harvey's Challenge,* in which the anchor would do all sorts of odd participatory sports challenges. "My devious news director knew this guy was coming in a few months so he stole the idea and we got it on the air first there."

Beasley's Challenges became immensely popular as Reece tried his hand at everything from skydiving to "backyard battle-ax tossing." His favorite bit was one on synchronized swimming. "There were these two petite white girls and me in the 'mermaid's pose' at the side of the pool," he recalls. With classical music playing, the camera showed one girl going in sideways—splash, then panned to the next—splash, then to "big ol' Beasley"—SPLASH. "My first few moves after that were perfect but then I lost it and almost drowned a couple of times. It was absolutely hilarious."

Of course, Reece was no stranger to oddball stunts. Back with the Giants he once was persuaded to race against a horse at the Monticello Raceway; having run a 4.42 40-yard dash in cleats in the heat outside in Dallas, he was clearly one of the league's fastest runners.

As the first man-versus-horse race since Jesse Owens did it, the matchup got coverage everywhere from *Sports Illustrated* to Warner Wolf's telecast. "I'd heard it was becoming a big event," Reece says, but it was when he and his teammates saw the giant "Beasley versus the Beast" signs at the raceway that he felt "straight fear." Fortunately, the horse, Super Kris, was one of the biggest losers in racing history and as a trotter was unused to starting from a standstill, and in a 100-meter race just didn't have enough time to catch Reece. "I won by a nose," he says, adding, "That night did more for making a name for me and for my career than anything else."

Reece, who is married with two sons, still loves challenging himself, as an avid golfer and fitness freak and as a musician too. From the age of six through high school he studied classical piano and he has taken lessons on and off through the years to keep his technique sharp. But he has always wanted to do more, to be a true musician, not just someone playing the music in front of him.

"In my dorm in North Texas, there'd be a guy playing Lionel Richie and all these beautiful girls would be hanging around, then I'd play Rachmaninoff and everybody would drift away till I was left with the odd-looking music major with glasses and her cello," he says.

So after years of trying to perfectly replicate others, he now plays jazz and blues, most of which he has written himself. In 2004, he played at a festival in Camden, performing original songs about Philadelphia sports, including "The Allen Iverson Blues" and a tune about old men reminiscing. "I felt like I'd completed some internal mission. Now I can entertain people," he says.

Reece has also sung the national anthem at NFL and NBA games and the Olympics. "It's very stressful," he says, explaining that he always thinks about Roseanne Barr, Carl Lewis, and other fiascos. "Every time I've done it I almost have a heart attack. I can't believe I've agreed to do it."

He kept pushing himself in his work too—after returning to Florida briefly in 1997, he made the jump to a major market in 1998 when he landed the job in Philadelphia. All along, he has also done network football work, either as an analyst or sideline reporter, first for NBC and now for CBS. But he speaks most fondly of being a boxing commentator for the 1992 Barcelona Summer Olympics, not because he is a huge boxing fan but because he knew so little about it. "It was an intellectual exercise," he says, recalling how NBC sent him boxes of books and he immersed himself in the learning experience.

In 2004, the Smarty Jones Triple Crown phenomenon was a similar fun, rewarding experience, especially since his family had owned horses in Texas, but he knew nothing about thoroughbred racing. Plunging into this new sport and journeying to the Preakness and Belmont Stakes was "the greatest month I've had since Barcelona."

Reece is also active in the community: he's on the local Boy Scout board and is an Eagle Scout and helps support Urban Promise, a Camden private school for underprivileged inner-city kids.

Although as a former Cowboy, Giant, and Buccaneer it might seem odd for him to say that on the whole he'd rather be in Philadelphia, Reece loves it there and wouldn't even give up that job to come back to New York at this point. "I plan to retire from this desk," he says. "For the first time in my life there's no carrot out there, nothing I'm fighting for."

But even when he does retire down the road, he'll certainly keep busy with all his other hobbies. Reece jokes that the "final chapter" in his life will be when he takes his music career on the road, winding up playing blues and jazz at a piano in a dimly lit lounge in Atlantic City, where some guy will look at him and ask, "Didn't you used to be Beasley Reece?"

Roy Simmons's greatest accomplishments as a New York Giant came far from the playing field and long after his playing days were over. For this popular offensive lineman showed true bravery when he became only the second former NFL player to openly declare he was gay, and then he went on to publicly admit he was HIV-positive. Since then Simmons has used the cachet of his status as an ex-Giant to urge men, especially black men, to stop living "on the down low"—leading a secret gay life while maintaining relationships with girlfriends or wives—and abusing drugs and to reach out to those struggling with some of the same issues he has faced.

"The key to grabbing people's attention is that I'm a former NFL player, so they'll listen and ask me what it was like," Simmons says, adding that he tells stories on himself about being filled with shame when stalwarts like George Martin would chastise him for showing up exhausted from his late-night life. "Then I put it out there and say, 'Guys, I'm telling on you—there are people dying out there and the victims are you and the people you love.' Hopefully I can plant a seed."

For Simmons, his brave actions in the last decade more than atone for a career in which he frittered away great potential on drugs, alcohol, and the pressure of keeping his double life a secret.

He had been keeping secrets since he was eleven, when he was raped by a neighbor, a respected member of the community, and no one in his family could talk about it or deal with it.

He told only one cousin, who told others in the family, yet no one spoke of the incident, confronted the man, or sought to get help for Roy. "I think everybody was in shock and their answer was, 'Don't say anything,'" he says. "The man was the mailman and back then he was like a government official—he was perceived as an authority with his blue uniform and stripes on the sides."

So Simmons pushed the memory down as far as he could and tried to resume his life as normally as possible. (He would say years later that he beat himself up psychologically after that, wondering if he would have otherwise been straight; unhappy with his homosexuality, for years he would need alcohol or drugs to be intimate with men, leading to many of his post-football problems.) Before the rape, Simmons says he had a normal, relatively happy childhood. His maternal grandmother, who worked as a maid, raised him and his five brothers and sister, but both his parents were in his life. (His grandmother, Loulabelle Simmons, also raised two other grandchildren.) His father was a bricklayer and his mother went north to work at different jobs. "She always sent money home to buy us clothes and she came back and forth and brought us up to New York each summer," recalls Simmons, the second oldest child. "We never really wanted for anything."

His older brother Larry was a straight-A student, and Roy strived hard to keep up. Although he had Bs mixed in with his As, he did well and loved school, even after the rape—from second grade on he had perfect attendance all the way through high school. He also did weight lifting to try to keep up with his older brother, learned to cook by watching his grandmother, and attended church and vacation Bible school each summer. Roy was also a star athlete, the high school football team's Most Valuable Player as an offensive lineman and the captain of the track team (he ran the 220 and 440 and threw the shot and discus) and a starter on the basketball team.

Major schools including the University of Southern California, Notre Dame, and Florida State recruited Simmons, but he wanted to stay closer to home and chose Georgia Tech. "It was right down to the wire with Florida State," he says, "but I didn't even really want to leave high school I had such a great time, and I didn't want to go far away from my family."

At college a friend named John Blue changed the warm and gregarious Simmons's nickname from "Horse" to "Sugarbear," and, says Simmons, "that just leaped out and got around." The team designed traps and sweeps to capitalize on Simmons's quickness on the line; by his junior year, Simmons "knew something was happening," and in his senior year "I knew that I could play on someone's team in the NFL."

That team was the Giants, who drafted Simmons in the eighth round in 1979. But Simmons had expected to go higher—he thinks the fact that he bounced around between guard, tackle, and nose guard to suit the team's needs hurt him—and was bitterly disappointed that night as he sat in his room surrounded by friends waiting for the phone to ring. "I said, 'Fuck the NFL, then I'm not playing,'" he recalls. (Simmons, a charming and polite man, immediately apologizes for using that language now, explaining that he's merely giving an honest report about what he said as a frustrated youth.)

The next day a friend knocked on the bathroom door while Simmons was showering to say the Giants were on the phone. "To hell with them," Simmons replied, but his friend insisted he go talk, and eventually he did, heading north to New Jersey.

"I didn't care what team I went to but I was very glad that I went there—I had gone up there to visit my mother and I had an aunt in Orange, whom I took up residence with till I got a place of my own," he says.

Even when Simmons got his own digs, he wanted to be surrounded by family, so he brought up his three younger brothers from Georgia. "Living conditions were not great down there," he says, adding that his mother and some cousins later joined them. There was some conflict, however, with Simmons playing the provider and father figure, occasionally butting heads with his mother and brothers. "I should have let my mother be head of the household," he says. Later he'd move into Jim Clack's old apartment, one loved by all the Giants for its magnificent views of the New York skyline.

But such proximity to the big city was also a bit of a problem for Simmons, who fell in with the partiers on the team and expended more energy on drinking, drugging, and living two lives—one heterosexual and one homosexual—than he did on training or taking care of himself.

"The drinking and drugs started as more of social thing, but there was so much stress and pressure from living on the down low, from saying, 'This is not happening to me,'" he says. "I just lost sight of everything. All that lying and cheating was wearing me out."

Back then, of course, the NFL didn't do much about drug use, whether it was cocaine or steroids, but Simmons doesn't blame the league or the Giants, who had him talk to their team psychologist, Joel Goldberg. "I could have gotten help if I had been more open," he says. "It was because of me putting on a façade—Dr. Goldberg was one of my favorite people. He gave me advice and he was there for me."

But Simmons wasn't ready to confront his demons, and his play suffered—in 1981 he lost his starting job. "Everything took its toll—with drugs and alcohol you can only handle so much," he says, adding that while he was bitter at the time, he understands now that the team was doing what it had to do.

Then in 1982, "it all came to a boil," and Simmons walked away from the game, citing "mental fatigue." He says team officials told him "no one leaves and comes back," but he felt he had no choice. Goldberg got him a job working as skycap supervisor for Pan Am, which he loved. He also kept working out, and the following season he decided he wanted to return to the Giants, even showing up a week early with all the rookies to prove how dedicated he was. Oops. Ray Perkins, who had been sympathetic, was gone as head coach. Bill Parcells, not known for his forgiving ways, was in. "He said to me, 'This is not a mission. You don't do what you did,'" Simmons says, adding that he "worked like hell" but was not given much of a chance, getting shuffled from guard to tackle without explanation and then cut.

Simmons latched on with Washington and did some blocking and performing on special teams. It was a special year—"I got to be a Hog and go to the Super Bowl"—but trouble was never far away. Simmons somehow invited two women and one man with whom he was romantically involved to the big event, and then he crumbled under the pressure, snorting cocaine the night before the game and driving around by himself snorting more afterward.

The Redskins cut Simmons the following year, but he hooked up with the Jacksonville team in the USFL. "I had been someone who said, 'The USFL doesn't really have NFL players,' and now I was eating my words," he says, adding that he was impressed by the quality of play and earned more in that league than he ever had in the NFL. But when the league folded and there was no football to provide at least some structure to his life, Simmons foundered worse than he ever had before.

"When I left football my drug habit took charge," he says. "I had numerous jobs where it caught up with me in terms of attendance or performance and I would have to resign. I had a really good job as a deputy clerk in a bankruptcy court that I really enjoyed—I saw myself staying there, but they asked me to resign so they wouldn't have to fire me."

Eventually the drug problem became so bad that it consumed Simmons, and he was essentially unemployable. Meanwhile, rumors of his sexual orientation were bubbling to the surface. So he disappeared. He lit out for San Francisco, hoping to find himself in such an openly gay community. But he was too far gone. "I was missing appointments and getting intoxicated and high every day. My funds were depleted," he says, adding that he was soon homeless, struggling just to keep a roof over his head by living in a welfare hotel. "I hit my bottom there."

But reaching the bottom forced him to reach toward the sunlight. He called an old friend, Jimmy Hester, who had worked as a busboy at a popular Giants hangout in New Jersey back during Simmons's playing days. "I told him, 'I need help. If I don't get out I'm going to die.'" Hester came through, getting Simmons into a rehab program, and then another a while later when Simmons relapsed.

Hester was then working as an entertainment publicist and he arranged for Simmons to come out of the closet in the most public forum possible, on *Donahue*. At that point, only one other former NFL player, Dave Kopay, had publicly come out. (More recently, Esera Tuaolo joined this small roster.)

"I was feeling good about myself then," he says. "Little did I know I wasn't ready for that. I didn't know the magnitude of it all, the calls, e-mails, and letters."

The event overwhelmed Simmons, who hadn't even gotten to tell his younger brother Gary before the show aired and who was devastated by the revelation. Other family members and ex-teammates acted as if the news couldn't be real. "Guys would say to me, 'You must have been hungover or had too much to drink—that wasn't really true.'"

Simmons then vanished from the public eye, saying now that the whole situation was too stressful. "I had to deal with so many different attitudes and to explain and explain and explain," he says. He did follow through on his original promise to Hester that he would give something back, however, and he worked for several years as a drug counselor at a halfway house on Long Island. "I knew their pain and struggles," says Simmons, who has acknowledged brief relapses of his own in 1999 and 2001. "It's a day-by-day process but I feel I changed people's lives."

Then in 1997, just before a trip to Israel, he went to his doctor complaining of sore throats. Among other things, the doctor administered an AIDS test. "I wasn't worried because I had just had one the year before," Simmons says. "Then he called me in and told me I was HIV-positive. My whole world went—my mind just left the room."

The first months of medication were very difficult as Simmons dealt with various side effects while trying to find the right cocktail, or mix of medications. He is fortunate, he believes, that he doesn't have an aggressive strain and his T-cell counts remain high years later. "I've learned that I'm living life on its terms," he says.

Still, even with the right cocktail, he often felt bloated and heavy; working in the halfway house at night and then going to Narcotics Anonymous meetings in the morning before trying to sleep during the day also threw him off. "I felt like I was dying a slow death," he says. "My ankles were swollen and I could hardly walk up a flight of stairs."

Again, it was Hester to the rescue. Hester, who had been diagnosed as HIV-positive in 2002, had discovered in 2003 a woman named Roni DeLuz, who runs a homeopathic retreat on Martha's Vineyard. In a twenty-one-day detoxification program, Hester shed pounds and regained a sense of well-being. So he persuaded Simmons, who was up to 286 pounds, to give it a try. After three weeks of juices, colonics, enemas, and antioxidants, Simmons was forty pounds lighter and also felt rejuvenated. (He and Hester now have a website selling the antioxidants and other related products.) "My life has truly been enriched," he says.

Simmons began attending church and singing in choirs, but losing weight and having his skin clear up also helped firm his resolve. He decided it was time to speak out about being HIV-positive, and so, on World AIDS Day in 2003, he did, becoming just the second pro team athlete to admit to being HIV-positive (besides Magic Johnson). And he didn't stop there—he began traveling around the country talking to AIDS groups, marching in AIDS walks, talking to people in drug programs, to the media.

After years of being so secretive about his drinking, drug use, sexuality, and then HIV-positive status, Simmons realizes that speaking out is good for him. "The speeches build my confidence and self-esteem," he says. "It's healthy for me to keep talking about it."

But he's not doing this for selfish reasons. He's doing it because he knows there are people struggling with drugs and with their own demons; he knows there are black men afraid to face up to their true selves in the macho world in which they live; he knows there are women being accidentally infected by the men they love.

"Somebody has to take a stand," he says. "I know some people are going to shy away, but this is an epidemic and we have got to let people know."

L ooking back, Scott Brunner believes he would have become a coach if he hadn't made it to the NFL; but, he adds, playing from 1980 to 1985 enabled him to "get it out of my system," leading to his second and third careers, in real estate and on Wall Street. Yet ultimately Brunner realized he could never get football completely out of his system, and that's why each autumn, Brunner also finds himself spending his Saturdays announcing college football on television.

The fact that football exerted such a strong pull over Brunner is not that surprising, given that his father has spent fifty years in the game—playing in college, then coaching and scouting in high school, college, and the pros, including fourteen years with the San Francisco 49ers and shorter periods with four other teams. In fact, Brunner's mother was athletic too, playing college basketball and then serving as a women's field hockey referee. Scott was the oldest of seven children, all of whom were athletic; life was a bit nomadic during Scott's childhood, moving around for his father's coaching jobs in Middletown, New York, then at Villanova, Temple, and Princeton, but there was always family and there was always sports.

The siblings weren't particularly competitive with each other, Brunner says, "since we all had our own little thing"—one sister played softball and one played field hockey; only one of his brothers also played quarterback, while the others played defense or wide receiver. Growing up, Brunner actually played more baseball and enjoyed it more than football, but by the time he'd finished his sophomore year in high school he'd "realized I wasn't going to be a baseball player."

So when the family moved to Lawrenceville, New Jersey, the next year, Brunner devoted more of his passion to football—although at 6'5", he also found a home on the basketball team and even carved out a niche for himself on the track team, where he ran hurdles as part of a long-term effort to improve his athletic development.

Brunner was enough of a student that several Ivy League colleges, along with the Naval Academy and the University of Delaware (whose coach knew John Brunner), recruited him. "I wanted something with a little more competitiveness on the football field than the Ivy League and I wasn't 100 percent sure I wanted to make the postgraduate commitment required by the Naval Academy," Brunner recalls, "and I knew Delaware had great fans and a great tradition from my father's coaching at Villanova and Temple."

So, it was off to Delaware to play football, although at that point, he says, the NFL "was not even a dream." It turned out that even Delaware football was a bit of a reach at first—after playing on the freshman team and then having one year of being red-shirted, Brunner, an accounting major, still had to spend two more years as a backup. Jeff Kolmo, who went on to the Detroit Lions, was the team's quarterback, and Brunner, who was still filling out, sat and learned—he especially learned the virtues of patience.

"I was a little gawky and hadn't really matured physically, so Jeff got the nod," Brunner recalls. "He never played poorly, so I was relegated to waiting it out."

Still, he refused to let go of his goals—when the coaching staff asked him to consider wide receiver, he replied, "I know I can play quarterback." He did consider transferring to another school, especially when he took one of his younger brothers around to visit Pennsylvania-based schools that were recruiting him—those coaches quickly expressed interest in having Scott come along too. But he remembered the advice his dad had given him. "He said, 'Make sure you go to a school where you will enjoy the experience even if you never get to play a single down,'" Brunner recalls, adding that he was happy with everything else about his time at Delaware.

And, finally, during his senior year Brunner got a chance to be happy about his playing time too. He was given a chance to show his stuff, and he made the most of the opportunity. Brunner threw for 2,401 yards and twenty-four touchdowns; Delaware had a 13-1 record and won the Division II playoffs, finishing off with an astonishing comeback against undefeated Youngstown State, rallying from being down 31–7 to a 51–45 win, with 20 seconds left. Brunner threw for 296 yards, including touchdown passes of 70 and 75 yards. (Ironically, Scott's younger brother Todd—the only other quarterback in the family—would later face a similar predicament. At Lehigh, he sat on the bench for three years before getting a chance, which he too seized, setting school records for touchdowns and total offense.)

That kind of performance appealed to the Giants, although they already had a young comer by the name of Phil Simms. Still, when Brunner was available in the sixth round, the Giants took him. Brunner says he was never fazed by the quarterback controversy stirred up by the media throughout his time with the Giants. "I kind of accepted it as normal—it wasn't until I left the Giants and played with other teams around the league that I realized the media situation here is not normal," he says.

His rookie year the team continued its losing ways, finishing at 4-12 in 1980. Although he says he never felt the burden of the Giants' recent history, he wasn't used to being on a losing team. And the next year, he helped turn the Giants around—when Simms went down with an injury, Brunner, less athletic but more cerebral than many quarterbacks, guided them to a surprisingly strong finish that catapulted them into their first playoff appearance since 1963.

"After everything I had gone through in college, I'd learned about having to wait and that you shouldn't expect multiple opportunities so you should just seize the moment," he says. "That helped me in the drive to the playoffs."

One highlight was going into Philadelphia near the start of that run and beating the first-place Eagles 20–10. "Nobody was considering us a contender at that point and we knocked them off in their place," he says. "For me, especially, growing up as an Eagles fan, that was very exciting. Then in the playoffs we went back and shocked them again."

Over the next two years Brunner received more opportunities to play—he threw 298 passes in the strike-shortened nine-game season in 1982 (with a 54.0 completion percentage) and 386 the following year. But in that 1983 season the whole team slumped, including Brunner, who completed less than half his passes and had only nine touchdowns and twenty-two interceptions—he was replaced after six games by Simms but was given his job back when

Simms got hurt, only to be benched in favor of Jeff Rutledge for the end of that 3-12-1 season.

With Rutledge and Simms around, Brunner was deemed expendable and was traded to the Denver Broncos the next season. But if competing for playing time with Phil Simms seemed tough, that was nothing compared to what was waiting for him there: John Elway. "He was only in his second year and hadn't proven himself, so the jury was still out," Brunner recalls. "But from the first day of practice when I saw him play I knew how good he would be."

Brunner sat on the bench as Elway broke out and led the team to a 13-3 season. "It was tough not to play, but it was fun being on an exciting and upbeat team at work every day," Brunner says.

In the off-season he was shipped to Green Bay, but during the 1985 preseason the Packers, blessed with an extra backup, packed him off to the St. Louis Cardinals, where he served in reserve. He was cut by St. Louis during the 1986 season and spent the next few weeks waiting for a general manager to call saying they needed his help. "It was the only year in NFL history that no quarterbacks get hurt," he says. Finally, the phone rang and on the other end was Giants front-office man George Young, with whom Brunner had become quite friendly while with the team.

"He said, 'Scott, I want to talk to you for a minute,' and I started getting all excited, but then George said, 'I'm thinking of trading for OJ Anderson, what do you think of him?' "

Although his hopes immediately deflated, Brunner did urge Young to make the deal, one which helped his old club tremendously. After the 1986 season, a few clubs did call, but by that point Brunner had started his own house-building business and he and his wife were getting set to have their second child. Considering that he had gone from New York to Denver to Green Bay to St. Louis in two years, he decided "you have to say enough is enough."

Brunner's business flourished until the early 1990s, when the Savings & Loan scandal aftermath, new laws, and a down real estate market made it very tough for small to midsize builders to stay afloat. He tried convincing his partners to reconfigure themselves into a group that bought and prepared land before selling it to large-scale developers for building, but when that failed he "followed the money trail" and ended up on Wall Street. Today he is vice president of equity sales for a Manhattan firm called Buckingham Research, overseeing seventeen analysts who make investing recommendations on everything from health care to chemical industries, which Brunner then takes to portfolio managers at large institutions.

"I enjoy it a lot," he says, adding that it's a lot like football because it requires tremendous preparation and a skill for anticipation and timing—just as a quarterback must throw the ball to a spot where his receiver will be, Brunner now must be able to see the "route" that a particular industry is running.

Football itself remains very much on his mind too. After retiring, Brunner did some radio announcing for Princeton, where his father had coached before moving on to Rutgers, where he spent eight seasons, before tiring of the workload and travel. Now Brunner has a deal announcing Northeast Conference games on regional television, but he generally doesn't have to work more than a half-dozen games each season.

"I don't do it for financial reasons—I do it because I enjoy it," he says, adding that he enjoys not only the football itself, but the people too. "On every staff, at every game, I know someone who I played with or against or worked under or someone who knows my dad," he says. "It's amazing how small the world is. It's great to get out and visit."

When Rob Carpenter was in third grade, he stood up in front of his entire family, shut the television off, and made an announcement.

Now there are a couple of things to understand here: first, this was a big family—Rob's dad, Robert Sr., came from a family of thirteen siblings, and many of them gathered regularly at the house in Lancaster, Ohio, to watch the Cleveland Browns play football. Second, while most of Ohio does not have what Carpenter calls "the Texas mentality" when it comes to a passion for football, the Carpenter clan certainly did. So if you were going to shut the Browns game off to address the crowd, you were putting a lot of pressure on yourself.

But that was okay with young Rob, who was "terribly intense." And so, in front of everyone, the boy declared: "I'm going to play professional football one day and you will all be watching me on TV."

Almost everyone in the room laughed, but Rob's dad did not. Carpenter says his father had been a pretty good football player in high school but never had any real opportunities beyond that. And while his dad didn't get to attend all his games or throw a football with him every day—he got up at 4:30 in the morning to go to work as a glazier (or glassworker) and often didn't return home till 6:30 in the evening—he was always especially supportive of Rob's dream. In the years to come, whenever the boy would get discouraged—which was natural for an undersized kid who never got to start in Peewee football or junior high school or even the first years of high school—his dad would remind him, "What about the NFL?" and the boy's determination would just grow. "Everything I did revolved around making it," he says. "I wanted to make my family proud of me."

The second oldest of five children, Carpenter would eventually prove himself right and reward his parents' encouragement with a ten-year career in the NFL, including a memorable 1981 season when he helped the Giants return to the playoffs for the first time in nearly two decades.

Looking back at a lifetime dedicated to the sport, Carpenter says he chose football as the sport to pour his heart into partially because it was the family's first love but also by the process of elimination. "I wasn't any good at any other sports, to be totally honest," he says, explaining that he knew he wasn't going to be the tallest or strongest or fastest or smartest athlete out there.

"Nobody ever thought I'd be very good at football either. I was very small. But football has a lot of intangibles—as a high school coach now I talk to my kids about heart, desire, and character," he says. "I can look them in the eye and say even if you don't get to play all the way till you're a junior in high school, you can still make it and play in college and maybe even the NFL."

Carpenter stuck it out even as his friends walked away from the game and he was passed over for playing time again and again. "I learned and I watched and I listened and I analyzed," he says, adding that the lack of instant gratification is sometimes harder to explain to today's football hopefuls.

When the opportunity finally arose, Carpenter made the most of it. He played defense in his junior year, but the next season he was the primary running back. In his senior year at Lancaster High School in 1972, he set a school rushing record with 1,556 yards, scored twenty touchdowns, and was named second-team all-Ohio, while attracting recruiters from as far away as California and as close to home as powerhouse Ohio State.

"I went to Miami of Ohio because it was known as the 'cradle of coaches,'" Carpenter says, explaining that outside of his father, his high school coaches were the men who influenced him the most, and he knew that if he didn't reach the NFL, he wanted to learn about what it would take to be a good coach.

In college, Carpenter continued his relentless drive toward the NFL. "Everything from the lifting to the running was gearing myself to make it," he says. "I didn't care if I was the first person picked in the draft or I had to go in as a free agent, I was going to make it happen somewhere, somehow."

Carpenter excelled, standing out as a two-time AP all-American and breaking the 1,000-yard mark in both his junior and senior years. But he says one moment in the 1977 East-West Shrine game was what propelled him into the pros. Carpenter, who didn't get into the game in the first half but played well enough in the second half to be named Outstanding Offensive Player, says he was trying to catch a short pass in the flat from Tony Dungy, but the ball was way off target and he had to lay himself all the way out to make a diving catch heading out of bounds. When he came skidding to a stop on the sidelines, he recalls, "the first thing I see are these bluish-purplish boots—which I later learned were made of ostrich—and I look up and there in a cowboy hat is Bum Phillips and he says, 'Hey, nice catch.'"

Phillips's Houston Oilers drafted Carpenter in the third round of the draft that year, but the rookie narrowly escaped an ignominious fate. The team was playing an exhibition game against the Super Bowl–champion Oakland Raiders, and five minutes before game time Carpenter learned he was being promoted from special teams to running back because of injuries to several veterans. That day Oakland routed Houston, but worst of all, three different Raiders returned punts for touchdowns. "After the game, Bum Phillips cut everybody on the punt special team," Carpenter says. "That could have been me."

In the middle of that rookie season, Carpenter became a starter, and he finished with 652 yards on 144 carries. For his effort he was named to the all-rookie team in the backfield with Tony Dorsett. "I said to myself, 'This is easier than I thought,'" he says.

But then the Oilers went out and drafted themselves another running back, and this one happened to be a combination workhorse-superstar: Earl Campbell. In the next three seasons Carpenter never carried the ball one hundred times in a year again, although he did contribute in other ways, catching forty-three passes for 346 yards in the 1980 season. "I was always looking for an edge, so I was a runner, a blocker, a receiver, and even a faker—doing it all helped me stay in the league," he says.

And Carpenter did indeed always find a way to contribute. His most memorable day came when Earl Campbell was too hurt to go against the San Diego Chargers in the playoffs. Carpenter, who was hurt as well, came off of crutches to gain 67 yards and spark the team to a 17–14 upset.

Still, Carpenter's diminishing playing time rankled him, as did the front office's tightfisted ways. Finally, when the owners fired

Bum Phillips, Carpenter began publicly demanding a trade. "I fought like heck to get traded and did some things I shouldn't have done," he says, adding that the firing of Phillips "was like Julius Caesar getting knifed in the back. I didn't want to be around after that."

At first the ownership refused to accommodate Carpenter, but four games into the 1981 season they sent him packing to the Giants for a third-round draft pick. "There was so much animosity at that point, the owners thought they were sending me to Siberia," he says, adding that while he was a bit wary of going to New York as a city and the lowly Giants offense, he "was excited just to go anyplace else."

Going to Texas from Ohio had been a culture shock, and coming to New York was another one. "In Texas everyone was real low-key and took long lunch breaks and talked slow and walked slow, but in New York you couldn't understand anyone, they were walking so fast and talking so fast," he says. Still, Carpenter made lasting friendships there and even thought about staying after retirement to work on Wall Street before deciding he wanted to return home to Lancaster to raise his family.

He also made himself right at home on the field. Carpenter's arrival was a turning point in Giants history. He gained 103 yards in his first game, against St. Louis—"I scored a touchdown and everybody was going crazy and I thought, 'This is good stuff'"— and transformed the team into winners. The team won each game in which he gained 100 yards (which happened five times) and was playing so well that Ray Perkins was able to persuade Jim Clack to come out of retirement when injuries left a gap at center.

Behind Clack's manhandling of Charles Johnson, Carpenter carved out a career-high 161 yards in the Giants' first playoff game since 1963, leading to a stunning upset over Philadelphia. "I was a reaction runner, a cut-back—I'd bounce and cut till I found something, and I told Clack I'd just be watching his behind and I'd go the other way," Carpenter says.

The next two years were cut short, first by a work stoppage and then by a knee injury in 1983, although Carpenter contributed nearly 900 yards in passing and rushing in that year. Then Carpenter bounced back strong in 1984, gaining 795 yards on 250 carries and 209 more on twenty-six catches, scoring a career-high eight touchdowns. It was an important year for the Giants as they bounced back from a disastrous 1983 season. But in 1985, with the emergence of Joe Morris, Carpenter's playing time was reduced, and then with the arrival of the bigger, stronger Maurice Carthon before the 1986 season, Carpenter knew it was time to move on. He skipped mini-camp and got himself traded to the Los Angeles Rams, but he hurt his back and played in only six games. "I needed major back surgery to continue playing and I didn't want that," he says.

Carpenter had some opportunities to be an assistant coach in college or in the NFL, but he knew the rigorous demands in terms of time and travel that those jobs required, with road trips, scouting, recruiting, and other never-ending demands.

"My dad never got to be around for all my events and I decided I was going to watch every game my kids were in," he says.

So Carpenter returned to Lancaster hoping to move on to the next dream, to become a high school coach, to pass on everything he'd learned about the game and about the intangibles that fueled his success. "I teach that good things happen when you hustle, and when your kids learn that and respond, it's an unbelievable feeling."

His first opportunity was at New Lexington High School, in a rural area near where his parents had bought a farm. "It was a terrible football program and nobody else wanted it," he says. Indeed, the team had gone 3-27 over the previous three years. But within three years Carpenter had built a powerhouse, winning the 1990 Muskingum Valley Championship, earning a state playoff berth. In 1992 he became athletic director, but he found the job less rewarding. "You don't really get to work with the kids," he says. "And it's not the same in terms of the thrill of victory and agony of defeat."

Then in 1995 a job opened as running back coach at his alma mater, Lancaster High. He jumped at the chance, only to be let go in 1996 due to school budget cutbacks.

But it worked out well for Carpenter, who went and coached his oldest son's junior high school team. "I didn't let Bobby play organized football till then," he says, explaining that he didn't want his son to be forced to follow his footsteps or have unfairly high expectations or even favoritism. "If he was going to play I wanted to make sure it was done the right way."

The team won two co-championships, and then in 1998 Carpenter took over as head coach for Lancaster High, a position he still holds. Two of his sons, Bobby and Jonathan, played for him and went on to play college ball, and two more, George and Nathan, are coming through, although Carpenter says all his kids are better overall athletes than he ever was. "My wife, Susie, is the swim coach and they're all good swimmers [Jonathan competed nationally], but if I jump into a pool I'm going to drown," he says.

By the time his youngest child is done with high school Carpenter will be fifty-five, at which point he says he'll either continue coaching high school or maybe even just coach younger children—he knows he'll be too old to begin a college or NFL career at that age. It's not something that particularly bothers him. "There are tradeoffs in every life and I'm very happy with the tradeoffs I made," he says.

Today, Carpenter can stand on Mount Pleasant, the highest point in Lancaster, and see where he grew up and where he lives and where he went to school and works. "I can basically see my whole life," he says. "It's kind of neat."

Brian Kelley works in the financial industry, with a nice office in the Chrysler Building and a lucrative job advising athletes how to manage their money. That's quite a long way from Lancaster, Texas, where Kelley spent part of his childhood without running water and electricity.

"It's amazing I got out," he says.

His transformation from one world to the other really came during his years with the New York Giants as Kelley blossomed from an unheralded late-round pick into a Pro Bowler on one of football's all-time greatest linebacking units—Kelley teamed with Brad Van Pelt, Harry Carson, and later a guy by the name of Lawrence Taylor to lead a Crunch Bunch defense that kept the Giants in games, even when the offense was incapable of winning them.

Kelley's first unit consisted of him and his two brothers, Richard and Arthur. The three became close after their parents ditched them, leaving the boys with their grandmother Mama Lil in small-town Texas south of Dallas. "We were dirt poor," he recalls. "We didn't have water or electricity. We never had a Christmas. Everything we had came from welfare."

The boys spent much of their time playing sports, and Brian and Richard, who were only a year apart, were especially close, often playing on the same teams. Then, Richard took on an even more important role in Brian's life during their tumultuous teenage years. One summer, the boys' mother, now remarried and living in southern California, brought them out for a visit. "Little did we know she wasn't sending us back," Kelley recalls, adding that they were distraught about leaving behind the only home they'd ever known and their Mama Lil for a woman they had seen once a year and a guy Kelley refers to as "the ultimate wicked stepdad." In that environment, Richard, more than ever, "was like a father to Arthur and me. He protected us."

Still, despite the turmoil, Kelley can look back and see that in the long term the move provided a crucial change, offering a better financial situation and the opportunity for the boys to find their way to college. Again, when it came to college, Richard paved the way: in junior high school back in Texas he had been a star quarterback—"he was a man already at that age"—in high school in Orange County he was all-county; he then went on to star at Cal Lutheran and eventually brought Brian along there.

"I never felt I was following in his footsteps in a bad way. I was always playing right alongside him going back to Little League. I think Arthur may have felt that about Richard and I though," he says. (Kelley says Richard has a successful construction business in Texas, and Arthur, after having "some problems" as a young adult, has straightened his life out and is running an air conditioner and heating company, also in Texas.)

At Sunny Hills High School, Brian Kelley played just about every sport—he played football, was a high jumper on the track team, and was the starting catcher for the baseball team, at least until his senior year, when a freshman walked on and took away his job. "It was Gary Carter," Kelley says, adding that he and Carter have remained friends to this day. "That ended my baseball career."

Best of all, Kelley played small forward on the second-ranked basketball team in the nation, a team that eventually lost to the top-ranked team from nearby Compton (which featured future NBA players like Larry Holyfield and Louie Nelson) in front of eighteen thousand people. "Basketball was my love," he says, adding that he took it so seriously that he gave serious consideration when his coach asked him not to play football that year because he might get hurt.

After high school, Kelley didn't know what to do. He had not had offers from major colleges and was considering possibly a junior college, but really, he says, "I had no clue." And then Richard stepped in, saying, "Why don't you come with me to Cal Lutheran?"

Brian went with him to Thousand Oaks and showed up in the coach's office, where he was enthusiastically welcomed. It proved a wise move for all involved. Kelley went on to become a two-time National Association of Intercollegiate Athletics (NAIA) all-American, setting a school record for interceptions with seventeen and even nailing a 68-yard punt.

While at Cal Lutheran, Kelley not only starred in football but also dabbled briefly in wrestling and discovered another new passion in rugby. "I only wrestled for one year when Richard dislocated his shoulders and they didn't have any other heavyweights," Kelley recalls, adding that the only wrestling experience he'd had was playing around in the house with his brothers. But Kelley proved a more-than-able replacement, winning the district and regionals and going to the nationals, where he lost in the second round. "Cal Lutheran was a small school—there were only eight hundred students—and they didn't have the funds to send me, so I had to go from dorm room to dorm room to try and raise the money to go."

Rugby proved a much more lasting interest. Rugby helped keep Kelley "in tremendous shape" and "improved my tackling, especially in one-on-one situations where you're the only guy who can drag a back down." Kelley eventually made his way onto the national team called the Grizzlies and later onto the Santa Monica rugby club, for whom he kept playing during the off-season in his years with the Giants.

But he did it without ever telling club officials back east and without the club ever finding out about it . . . until the day in 1980 when his team won the national championship and Kelley scored the winning points. "The next day there were pictures of me in the paper and Ray Perkins saw them and called me up. He said, 'Who told you you could play rugby?' and I said, 'No one said I could, but no one said I couldn't.'" Perkins told him in no uncertain terms his rugby career was over and that he was to pack his bags and immediately move back east where the Giants could keep an eye on his off-season workouts. "Within a month I was living in Upper Saddle River in New Jersey," he says.

Of course, rugby always took a backseat to football, even back in college. In his junior year, Kelley, along with his brother, was a key component of the Kingsmen's NAIA Division II national championship team. Before 1971, Cal Lutheran had been passed over for the playoffs six consecutive seasons despite averaging nine victories under coach Bob Shoup. But in that year, they'd go 8-0-2, coming from behind to upset heavily favored defending champ Westminster 30–14 for the title. Westminster, which hadn't lost in two seasons, should have been the host, but the weather in Pennsylvania was expected to be freezing, so the NAIA scheduled it on Cal Lutheran's sunny home turf. Still, they took a 14–7 lead in the fourth quarter before Lance Calloway returned a kickoff 93 yards for a Cal Lutheran touchdown, Mike Sheppard scored a 14-yard touchdown run on a fake field goal, Richard Kelley kicked a 25-yard field goal, and then Brian Kelley, who would later be selected "back of the game," returned an interception 33 yards for a touchdown.

In part because the daughter of famed *Los Angeles Times* sports columnist Jim Murray went to Cal Lutheran, the school's season garnered a surprising amount of media attention, enabling the players and school to make a name for themselves. "We got tremendous pub out of that—we were even on television," Kelley recalls. "It was quite an experience."

By that time, Kelley, who was majoring in mathematics, believed he had a shot at the NFL, not only because of the exposure and experience of playing for Cal Lutheran but also because of his summer job there. Each summer, rather than go home to his mother and stepfather, Kelley would stay in Thousand Oaks and work for the Dallas Cowboys, who held their training camp there. Although he mostly did gopher work, driving players and the media to and from the airport, Kelley says the job "helped me tremendously"—it gave him confidence that he could make it in the NFL and gave him a sense of what to expect when he finally did find himself in a pro camp.

Even after Cal Lutheran overscheduled itself following the championship season and muddled through a 5-5 year, Kelley thought he was going to be drafted by the Cowboys, which would have provided a sort of homecoming for him back in Texas. "They knew me and told me I'd probably go in the third or fourth round," Kelley says. But the Cowboys passed over him one time too many and the Giants snatched him up, even though they had chosen a linebacker named Brad Van Pelt as their number one pick.

"I didn't see myself making it there," Kelley recalls. "They had a pretty strong unit and they had chosen Brad. But I played mostly special teams in the preseason and I played well. Then Brad pulled his groin and Pat Hughes hurt his ankle and I intercepted a Terry Bradshaw pass and ran it for a touchdown at the end of preseason."

Kelley made the team but thought he'd mostly play special teams; although he and Van Pelt would not become close friends until the following year, he found himself a mentor in Jack Gregory, who took him under his wing and also took him out partying. The night before Kelley's first NFL game, in Cleveland, he was out till 4 a.m. with Gregory and the veteran's friends—the next day he found out he was starting only when the lineups were announced. "Jack said, 'Come on, rook, you've gotta play,'" Kelley says, adding that he was so filled with nervous energy that he overcame his exhaustion to make fifteen tackles.

Still, it wasn't until Marty Schottenheimer was brought in as a defensive coach that Kelley felt he really came to understand the game. "I owe a lot to him. He taught Harry (Carson), Brad, and I how to study film," Kelley says. Soon Kelley was able to read what play the other team was going to run just by his understanding of the situation and how they lined up. He became one of the game's premier defensive signal callers, yelling audibles to his fellow linebackers.

But he adds that he was forced to be a good student because he lacked the speed of a Van Pelt, a Carson (who came in 1976), or later an "LT" (who arrived in 1981). "I had to know where the ball was going before the ball got there," he says. The others had more natural skill and came to rely on Kelley to do the thinking. "We'd break the huddle and Brad would say, "What am I supposed to be doing?' And LT would say, 'What should I be doing?' And then right before the snap Harry would say, 'Brian, should I blitz?' They knew they could trust me."

The chemistry the men shared and their remarkable defensive success made the Giants' struggles more bearable for Kelley during the 1970s, as the offense floundered and the team made a succession of poor draft picks and coaching hires. Even later, when Van Pelt, Carson, and Taylor grumbled publicly, Kelley kept his peace. "I never asked to be traded anywhere, I was just happy to be playing in the NFL. I never had the luxury they had," Kelley says.

Kelley missed much of 1980 with a bad knee injured during a preseason game against the New York Jets and aggravated soon after in Philadelphia. But in 1981 he bounced back with 186 tackles and two key fumble recovers as the team returned to the playoffs for the first time since 1963. "I remember it really hit me when we were in Philadelphia after winning the playoff game and realizing we were going on to San Francisco and I said, 'I don't believe this.'"

But the Giants stumbled after that, and Kelley's age started showing. When Bill Parcells was promoted from defensive coordinator to head coach, Kelley says, Parcells offered him the defensive coordinator position, but Kelley still felt he could contribute on the field and he balked at going from his $170,000 annual salary to $40,000 income of a coach. The position went instead to a young Bill Belichick. But the 1983 season was a 3-12-1 disaster and, soon after, Parcells began remaking his defense, trading Terry Jackson along with Van Pelt and Kelley.

"I got a call from a friend of mine who was a scout who said, 'Did you know you're on the waiver list?'" Kelley recalls. He went to Parcells, who acknowledged it and asked if he wanted to be traded to one of the four teams that expressed interest. "I said, 'Listen, if you don't want me, then trade me.'"

Kelley had recently been divorced and chose to go to the San Diego Chargers to be closer to his children, although he ended up not making the team and then moving back to New Jersey, where he still lives today. He was a bit hurt because Parcells had gathered his linebackers upon taking the job and told them he owed his hiring to their superior play and he'd never forget that. Still, Kelley knew on some level Parcells was right. "I was running a 5.2 40 and my knees were shot," he says. "Bill grabbed the bull by the horns and it worked out for him and the Giants."

Kelley would have still seemed a logical choice for some coaching role given his cerebral approach to the game, but he says two factors moved him away from that kind of job. "I'd been playing football since I was eight years old and I wanted to see if I could do something else with my life," he says. "I was a mathematics major—I was not an idiot."

But Kelley also says it was a lifestyle choice, explaining that he didn't have the do-anything-and-everything, round-the-clock mentality that seems to be required for coaches. "I wanted to enjoy life with my family and have time on my own. Coaches work their asses off—it's amazing, the hours they put in."

Kelley dabbled in several businesses over the next two decades, from a limousine service to a travel agency that he co-owned with other former NFL players for three years. One venture, the Satin

Dolls Lounge, which Kelley opened in 1989 in Lodi, New Jersey, later brought him some grief when state investigators began looking into payments Kelley made to Vincent Ravo, a convicted felon and reputed mobster who used to hang with the Giants at a bar called The Bench. (Ravo's connections would also later cause legal trouble for Taylor, who was a close personal friend.) Kelley says the state was essentially out to prove that Ravo was the secret owner (he was not allowed to have a liquor license himself) and that was reflected in Kelley's payments to him, but Kelley testified that it was payment for help with renovations. "It was not a big deal," Kelley says today. "It was all a bit ridiculous."

Kelley began working as a sports agent for a group called Bienstock Sports, but later, as the agent business was changing, he was talking to his financial advisor Peter Borowsky about the huge salaries players were earning and about how they had no one to manage the money. So in 2001, the men formed Borowsky and Kelley Sports Group under the Prudential Securities umbrella (now Prudential is owned by Wachovia Securities). The business has gone extremely well, with the men handling twenty-five to thirty football, baseball, and basketball clients. "We're even looking into moving into entertainers," Kelley says.

But no matter how much time he spends in a corporate office, no matter how far removed from his playing days Kelley is, he still shares a special bond with his linebacking mates. Every year, Carson, Taylor, Van Pelt, and Kelley go to the Pro Bowl together and do autograph sessions together. But Kelley, who also has hosted an annual golf tournament in Thousand Oaks to raise athletic scholarship money for Cal Lutheran, says it's not all fun and money—the four men recently went to Pueblo, Mexico, where they did volunteer work helping build houses for Habitat for Humanity.

"It was pretty impressive seeing the work," he says, adding that they got to have lunch with former president Jimmy Carter. "The four of us love hanging out together, but we also try to give something back." For someone like Kelley, who has come so far from his roots, the opportunity to help others has a special resonance.

Looking back" is a favorite phrase of Brad Van Pelt. One of the more reflective, thoughtful men to play linebacker, the five-time Pro Bowler spends a lot of time "looking back" and thinking about what he should have done differently, wondering what might have been had he chosen a different path.

Most of the time, though, after giving it enough thought, Van Pelt is pretty happy with the way things turned out in his career. There is one thing, however, that more than any other he really wishes he could have done differently.

"I wish I could have retired a Giant," he says, explaining that he regrets forcing the team to trade him—not so much because he missed out on the glory of the Super Bowl years but because it was only after wandering to three teams in four years afterward that he came to truly appreciate what he had in New York. "I then realized how special the Maras are and that the Giants are the greatest organization in professional sports."

The most talented player of those 1970s teams almost didn't end up on the Giants to begin with, coming close to signing with the Cardinals instead—the baseball Cardinals, that is. Growing up in Owosso, Michigan, Van Pelt was a standout in football, basketball, and baseball. In fact, after high school the Detroit Tigers, his hometown team, drafted him. "The dream was dangling out there in front of me," he says, "but my dad and mom had other thoughts. College came first."

The good thing was that Michigan State football coach Duffy Daugherty wanted Van Pelt so badly he said he'd give him time to go out for baseball and basketball too. Van Pelt, who had played both free safety and quarterback in high school, enrolled, thinking he'd be the next Michigan State quarterback. Freshmen weren't eligible to play on the varsity, and in his sophomore year he suddenly realized he'd be stuck as the third-team quarterback without getting a real shot to play.

"There were much better opportunities to play on defense," he recalls, adding that as the backup free safety he got a chance to make a name for himself almost right away.

In the first game, out in Washington, with the team getting routed, Daugherty stuck Van Pelt in for the fourth quarter and the youngster nabbed an interception and made a few good tackles, earning the starting job for the home opener. In that game, Van Pelt came up with three interceptions "and that was the end of me as a quarterback."

Still, at that point, Van Pelt says, "I really felt baseball was going to be my best opportunity to play pro sports. I didn't understand until junior year that I could make it in pro football."

Then suddenly, the following season, his dream was almost thrown off course again. Daugherty was getting pressured from alumni and knew he might get fired; desperate for an infusion of new life in the offense, he called in Van Pelt and said he might switch him to quarterback. "For forty-eight hours, my dream was a possibility again," Van Pelt says. "But Daugherty, who was like a second father to me, called me back in to his office and said, 'You had a good year last year. I'm not going to jeopardize your chances for this.'"

Van Pelt was a little disappointed but realized that he probably wouldn't be able to do enough in one year to get drafted as a quarterback. "Looking back at what he did, with his job on the line," Van Pelt says he is touched that Daugherty put the player's future ahead of his own. (Daugherty was indeed let go after that year.)

But in his senior year the co-captain was a consensus all-American and the first defensive back ever to earn the Maxwell Award for the top collegiate player, enhancing his status with NFL teams. The Giants made him their top pick . . . but the St. Louis Cardinals, inspired by his eighty-four strikeouts and 100-mile-per-hour fastball, drafted him as a pitcher. While the two offers were so close in dollars that Van Pelt jokes that the Giants and Cardinals must have colluded, two factors pushed Van Pelt into football: "I enjoyed the team aspect more in football. Baseball, particularly if you're a pitcher, is more of an individual sport. There's something about coming together as a team and pulling something off that's special," he says. Additionally, baseball meant the minor leagues and a potentially long struggle just to see if he could make it, whereas with football he'd be in the NFL right away. "And if football didn't work out, I'd be young enough still to try baseball."

So Van Pelt signed with the Giants. But he did it a little too soon—because he signed during the school year, he was ineligible for other sports and couldn't pitch or play hoops his senior year. "Looking back, that's one of two major mistakes I'd really like to do over," he says, explaining that he missed out on the chance to play basketball one last time with some of his closest friends and to become Michigan State's first nine-letter man in more than three decades. (However, he acknowledges that if he had played those sports and gotten injured, ruining his football career, then he would have looked back on that decision with regret.)

After finding himself on the back of the *Daily News* and getting tabs picked up for him all around town, Van Pelt's first year was filled with frustration. For starters, he had to learn a new position: linebacker. The veterans were quick to stick it to this $100,000 kid. On the first day, Van Pelt had to try to get past Bob Tucker and two blocking dummies to a running back in something called "The Nutcracker Drill." Instead, Tucker "drove me back 11 yards and pinned my shoulders to the ground. I have never been so embarrassed." (Tucker, "who later turned out to be a tremendous friend," did explain afterward that as a linebacker Van Pelt needed to get lower than he ever did as free safety.)

Then Van Pelt tore his groin muscle during the exhibition season and was shelved till near the season's end, when he was named the backup tight end (although he never played a down there) and also was stuck into a game at strong safety. Meanwhile, the special treatment ended, and many of the people who had sidled up to him early on just faded away. Van Pelt went home on the verge of quitting. Indeed, the New York Mets drafted him after the season, thinking he might change his mind about baseball.

Looking back, as he is wont to do, Van Pelt says that, in some respects, "it was probably one of the greatest years of my life—that was the first time I had ever really failed. I learned about myself and about who my real friends were." And when he did become a star, those lessons helped him keep an even keel.

When Van Pelt returned, there was a new coach—the defensive-minded Bill Arnsparger had replaced Alex Webster—and a picket line. The NFL players were on strike, but Van Pelt soon decided that he had to break with them or "I may not be around to benefit from it." Some veterans understood, while some derided him as a scab, but meanwhile the youngster got one-on-one linebacking tutorials with the new coach. Besides Arnsparger, Van Pelt says he owes his success to the advice and help of Marty Schottenheimer, who later came in as defensive coordinator, and sharp-minded fellow linebacker Brian Kelley.

Even after establishing himself in the NFL, Van Pelt threw himself into his job like a man on the verge of losing it—an approach that traced back through his college days to his childhood. "I never, ever felt comfortable. I always lacked self-confidence," he says. "My father used to say, 'No matter how good you think you are or how good you are, there's always someone better.' And that was always in my mind—I was always waiting for someone better to come along . . . even after making it to the Pro Bowl." (Although he says that outlook helped push him to become a star, he took a very different tactic with his own children, "preaching that they should be confident and believe in themselves.")

While Van Pelt got better and better—eventually tying Sam Huff for the team linebacker record with eighteen interceptions—the Giants didn't. Since its last championship game in 1963, the franchise had fallen and fallen and fallen—in Van Pelt's first eight years the team's record was 33-85-1. This was the era that was remembered for the Pisarcik Fumble in 1978 and the airplane banner declaring, "Fifteen years of lousy football: We've had enough."

During the worst of it Van Pelt asked about being traded home to the Detroit Lions, but eventually he came to see himself as a Giant; although he never accepted losing, he was praised in the press for handling the situation well. Of course, when they finally made the playoffs in 1981 Van Pelt was injured at the season's end and missed the big game. Then the team finally appeared to be breaking through in 1983 and was being picked for first or second place under new coach Bill Parcells. But instead the club collapsed in a dismal 3-12-1 season, and Van Pelt's relationship with Parcells soured.

"I'd had a great relationship with him when he was defensive coordinator, but he became different as head coach—he couldn't be as close to us, but he was a son-of-a-gun to be around," Van Pelt recalls.

All through those losing seasons, Van Pelt had prided himself on playing his hardest no matter how dire the situation. But by the last two or three games of 1983, Van Pelt found himself one of the last ones out onto the field, unable to get motivated. "I had lost my edge. I didn't want to go out there," he says.

Van Pelt was coming off a season where he was fourth on the team with eighty-two tackles, including three quarterback sacks, but he thought he needed a fresh start and asked for a trade. Parcells said he'd feel better after a month at home. But Van Pelt didn't change his mind. Parcells still said no. Van Pelt grew angry and went into Parcells's office and mouthed off, complaining that he was tired of new head coaches every few years and wanted to play for a contender coached by a Chuck Noll or Tom Landry. "He told me to get out of his office, but I can't repeat how he said it," Van Pelt says.

Soon after, the Giants drafted linebacker Carl Banks (from Michigan State no less) and Parcells shipped Van Pelt off to Minnesota, a rebuilding team with a first-year coach, Les Steckel, having replaced the legendary Bud Grant and imposed a boot camp mentality on the Vikings. "I think Parcells made an example of me," Van Pelt says.

This time, however, Van Pelt would not be shoved around. He refused to report to Minnesota, sitting out half the season back home at the Club Ten golf course he owned in Owosso. Finally, at the trading deadline Al Davis acquired him for the Los Angeles Raiders. When Davis told him he'd been trying to get him for three months, Van Pelt realized that both Parcells and the Vikings had shafted him.

Life with the Raiders was good. "They were a veteran team with a relaxed atmosphere. It was like night and day. I had a lot of fun there," Van Pelt says.

But while he also loved being on a winning team—the club went 11-5 and 12-4, twice reaching the playoffs—it felt hollow. "There was something missing," he says. "I cheated myself by getting traded to a winner. I took the easy way. It would have been so rewarding to see it through all the way with the Giants; it would have been so much more special to be part of it when it turned around.

"I wish I had kept my mouth shut and played my whole career

with the Giants," Van Pelt says. "At least I should have come back and played one game with them so I could have retired as a Giant. The Mara family has been nothing but tremendous to me over the years."

After the Raiders, Van Pelt spent one year in Cleveland playing for Schottenheimer. Although he didn't get much playing time and was stuck largely on special teams, he did go almost all the way to the Super Bowl before being derailed by the Denver Broncos' amazing comeback in the AFC championship—"we would have played the Giants, if it hadn't been for John Elway and The Drive," he says.

Schottenheimer asked him to return, not to play much but to help the Browns' new draft picks, but Van Pelt, whose wife and four children had stayed behind in California the previous season, instead chose a job selling health insurance he'd been offered by a contact he'd met at a Santa Barbara golf tournament run by Duffy Daugherty. "The job was not going to be there a year later, and there are worse places to be than Santa Barbara," he says. Of course, the Browns' pick Mike Junkin hurt his shoulder and played only four games, so Van Pelt probably would have played plenty. "Looking back, I should have gone to Cleveland." (Believing he's "on the fence" as a Hall of Famer, Van Pelt says that fifteenth year might have helped . . . of course, staying with the Giants and reaching that Super Bowl would have helped even more.)

After three years the insurance company folded and Van Pelt helped open the Duffy Doherty Gridiron Grill, a sports restaurant in Santa Barbara. That too lasted three years, but it was not a success by any means. "It's a long story that I don't want to get into," Van Pelt says. "I learned a lot about the business world. I got kind of taken, big time."

Then it was on to a computer company near San Francisco, but when Van Pelt and his wife divorced, he moved back to Michigan to be with his children. "Divorce is not fun for anyone," he says. "I feel like I let my kids down."

While there he decided to finish college—he had left a few credits shy—"to show the kids their old man could do it after talking about it for all those years." Afterward, he taught phys ed for a year at East Lansing High School, then worked as a substitute.

These days, he's semi-retired and would only work if the job gave him the flexibility to spend time traveling to be with his sons, particularly Bradlee, who was drafted as a quarterback by the Denver Broncos in 2004. "I don't need to make a tremendous amount of money. I just want to be the best parent I can be," he says.

(Bradlee had gone to Michigan State as a quarterback but, like his father, was not given a real opportunity and was told to switch to defense. "If they had told me to play offensive tackle I would have said, 'Okay, I'll try,'" Van Pelt says. But after years of listening to his father preach self-confidence and wonder aloud about "what might have been," Bradlee refused, instead transferring to Colorado State, where he became a star quarterback, leading the team to three straight bowl games and becoming just the fourth college quarterback to pass for 5,000 yards and rush for 2,000.)

Those feelings have been particularly acute since the death of his oldest son, Arnold, in 2001. (Van Pelt's four sons were all named for family members or close friends—Arnold was named for his father, while the youngest, Brian Wellington Van Pelt, is named in part for former roomie Brian Kelley and for Mara.) Arnold, who was living in Boulder, Colorado, liked to live on the edge—whether it was bungee jumping, diving from bridges, or partying with friends. And he wanted to be his own man, so after he was hit by a car while riding a bike he did not ask his parents for help paying for hospital bills but instead got his ribs wrapped and took some painkillers a friend gave him. Then he went to a party celebrating the Colorado Avalanche Stanley Cup triumph and—given that he was taking unprescribed medication—drank too much. He died in his sleep that night.

Now with second-oldest Brett back in Santa Barbara and both Brian and Bradlee in Colorado, Van Pelt, who remains in Michigan where his brothers and mother are, wants to be free to travel to be with them.

"I feel I had two great parents, but I'm at an age where I'm giving myself a grade as a parent and I think I could have done a lot more, so for the last half of my life my goal is to just be there for my children," he says. "I think I'm on the right track."